the 50 best

country inns & small city hotels in Germany, Austria and Switzerland

by Robert Bestor & Tom Bestor

A pocket publication of *GEMüTLICHKEIT*
The travel letter for Germany, Austria and Switzerland

Composition and layout by Paul Merschdorf, Merschdorf & Associates, Inc., Oakland, Ca 94610.

Hotel illustrations by Brad Hicks.

Copyright © 1989 by Upcountry Publishing, 2892 Chronicle Avenue, Hayward, CA 94542. Telephone 415/538-0628.

All rights reserved. No part of this book may be reproduced or transmitted in any form by any means, electronic or mechanical, including photocopying and recording, or by information storage and retrieval system, except as may be expressly permitted by the 1976 Copyright Act or in writing to GEMüTLICHKEIT, c/o Upcountry Publishing, 2892 Chronicle Avenue, Hayward, CA 94542.

Manufactured in the United States of America.

ISBN 0-9625238-0-1

CONTENTS

INTRODUCTION 5

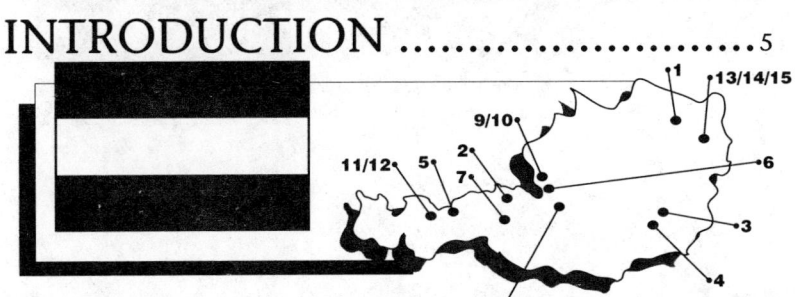

AUSTRIA 7

CITY	MAP #	HOTEL NAME	PAGE

DÜRNSTEIN
    1 – Schloß Dürnstein 9
ELLMAU
    2 – Hotel der Bär 11
SEBERSDORF
    3 – Schloß Obermayerhofen 13
OSWALD BEI GRAZ
    4 – Schloß Plankenwarth 15
INNSBRUCK
    5 – Romantik Hotel Schwarzer Adler 17
OBERALM BEI HALLEIN
    6 – Schloß Haunsperg 19
PINZGAU
    7 – Jagdschloß Graf Recke 23
OBERTAUERN
    8 – Hotel Kohlmayr 25
SALZBURG 27
    9 – Hotel Goldener Hirsch 27
    10 – Pension Wolf 29
SEEFELD
    11 – Gartenhotel Tümmlerhof 31
    12 – Hotel Lärchenhof 33
VIENNA 35
    13 – Römischer Kaiser 37
    14 – Kaiserin Elisabeth 39
    15 – Hotel König von Ungarn 41
    Looking for Mr Goodbeisel 42

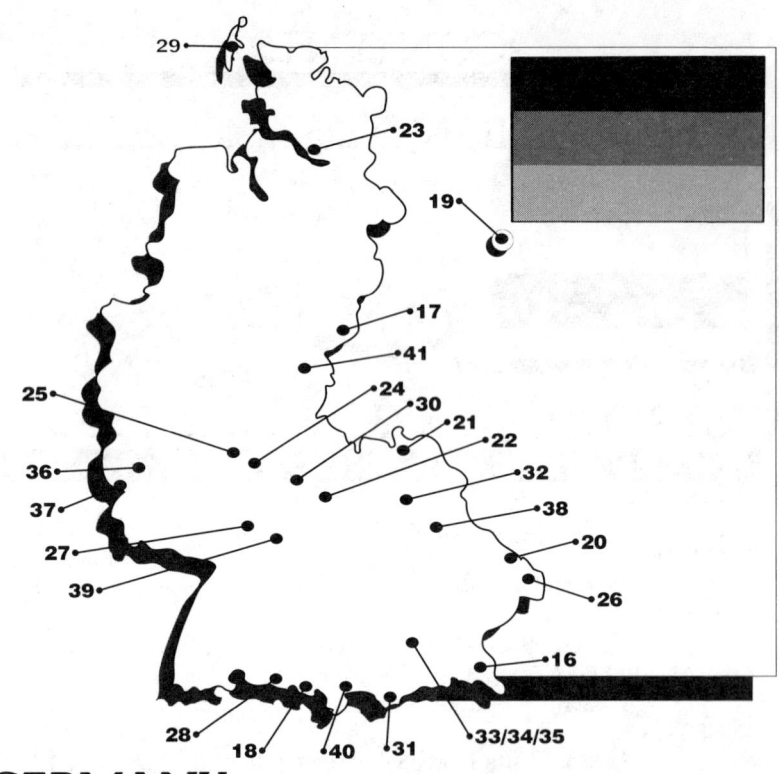

GERMANY 45

| CITY | MAP # | HOTEL NAME | PAGE |

BAD REICHENHALL
    16 – Hotel Hofwirt 47
BAD SACHSA
    17 – Harzhotel Romantischer Winkel 49
SCHACHEN
    18 – Strand-Hotel Tannhof 53
BERLIN 54
    19 – Hotel Am Zoo 55
BODENMAIS
    20 – Hotel Andrea 57
COBURG
    21 – Hotel Blankenburg 59
FRICKENHAUSEN
    22 – Waldhotel Polisina 61

The 50 Best Country Inns & Small, City Hotels

GERMANY, continued

CITY	MAP #	HOTEL NAME	PAGE

HAMBURG
23 – Hotel Abtei 63
HANAU (STEINHEIM)
24 – Hotel Birkenhof 65
KÖNIGSTEIN
25 – Hotel Sonnenhof 67
HOHENAU
26 – Romantik Hotel Bierhütte 69
HEIDELBERG
27 – Hotel Hirschgasse 71
MEERSBURG 73
28 – Villa Bellevue 73
KEITUM/SYLT 75
29 – Hotel Benen Diken-Hof 75
MARKTHEIDENFELD
30 – Hotel Anker 79
MITTENWALD
31 – Berghotel Latscheneck 81
MUGGENDORF
32 – Hotel Feiler 83
MUNICH 87
33 – Hotel Prinzregent 89
34 – Hotel Exquisit 91
35 – Hotel An der Oper 93
NEUMAGEN DHRON
36 – Gutshotel des Weingutes 97
TRIER
37 – Petrisberg 99
NÜRNBERG 101
38 – Weinhaus Steichele 103
FRIEDRICHSRUHE
39 – Wald und Schoßhotel Friedrichruhe 107
PFRONTEN-DORF
40 – Hotel Bavaria 109
SPANGENBERG
41 – Schloß Hotel Spangenberg 111

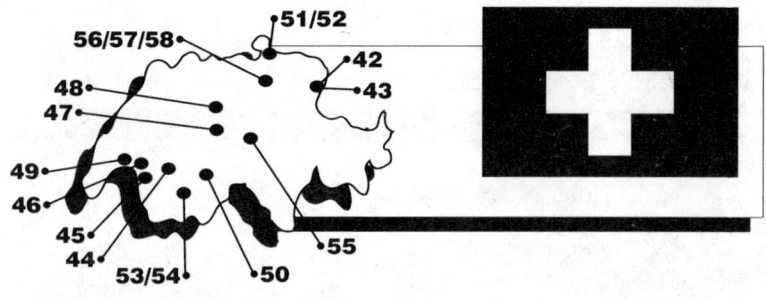

SWITZERLAND 115

CITY	MAP #	HOTEL NAME	PAGE

APPENZELL 117
    42 – Hotel Hecht 117
    43 – Romantik Hotel Säntis 119
CHATEAU-D' OEX 121
    44 – Hostellerie Bon Accueil 123
GLION-SUR-MONTREUX 125
    45 – Hotel Victoria 125
CHERNEX
    46 – L'Auberge De Chernex 127
ISELTWALD 129
    47 – Chalet Du Lac 129
LANGNAU IM EMMENTAL
    48 – Landgasthof Hirschen 133
LAUSANNE 135
    49 – Hotel La Residence 135
LEUKERBAD
    50 – Les Sources des Alpes 139
STEIN AM RHEIM 143
    51 – Hotel Chlosterhof 143
    52 – Hotel Rheinfels 145
VERBIER 149
    53 – Hotel de la Poste 149
    54 – Rosalp 151
WILDERSWIL
    55 – Hotel Bären 153
ZÜRICH 155
    56 – Hotel Florhof 157
    57 – Hotel Tiefenau 159
    58 – Hotel zum Storchen 161

in Germany, Austria & Switzerland

Acknowledgments

By a factor of about 10, this simple little book — our first — was a bigger project than first envisioned. We would like to express our thanks to a handful of people who were intimately involved in making the "Fifty Best" a reality.

Lois Bestor and Elizabeth Bestor were unpaid proof readers and dispensers of common sense. Their comments always seemed to start with the question, "Do you really want to say this?" Invariably we didn't and yet another embarassing *faux pas* was averted.

Joe Lustenberger, of the Swiss Tourist Office in San Francisco, is at the top of an extremely short list of people who took us seriously in 1986 when we launched *Gemütlichkeit* – The Travel Letter for Germany, Austria and Switzerland. His help and guidance in those days when we could write our list of subscribers on a cocktail napkin won't be forgotten.

The amazing Paul Merschdorf, who designed and laid out every page of the book, including the front and back covers and the maps, kept the whole project moving forward; and, because he cares that things are done right and is a friend, gave us major league graphics on a minor league budget.

The Authors

INTRODUCTION

In three countries where excellence in small hotels is the norm, it is difficult to pick a list of only 50 (actually there are 58 in this book). We have not visited all the good hotels in these three countries and qualities we deem important others may disregard. Thus, the reader may not find his favorite hotel, or disagree with the inclusion of certain ones he or she has tried and found wanting.

The 58 hotels in this book are not best in the traditional sense. The term, in fact, is probably misleading. It connotes luxury and expense; not entirely what we had in mind in choosing the hotels for this book. The establishments presented here are "best" for a variety of reasons. To be sure, some are both luxurious and expensive. For example, the Benen Diken Hof on the island of Sylt off the north coast of Germany, and Les Sources des Alpes in Switzerland, are among the world's finest small hotels and charge accordingly.

Presented here, however, are the 58 best recommendations we could make to a good friend or family member who wanted to spend moderately most of the time, splurge occasionally, but, most of all, wanted to be well off the beaten path and experience that special brand of hospitality and warmth we think is unique to the small hotels and inns of Germany, Austria and Switzerland.

Robert H. Bestor, Jr.

Thomas P. Bestor

August, 1989

The 50 Best Country Inns & Small, City Hotels

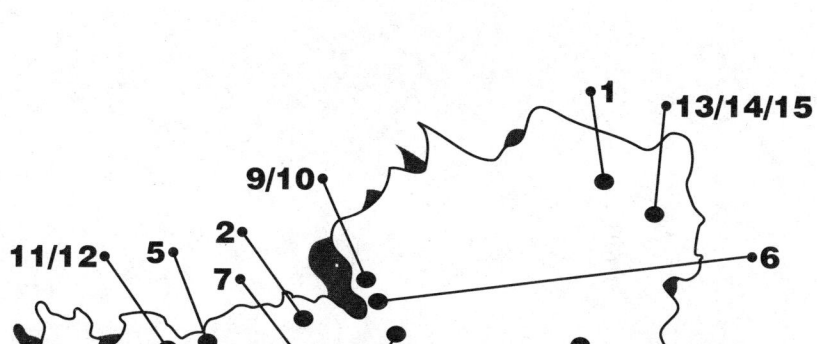

AUSTRIA

1 Schloß Dürnstein
2 Hotel Bår
3 Schloß Obermayerhofen
4 Schloß Plankenwarth
5 Schwarzer Adler
6 Schloß Haunsperg
7 Jagdschloß Graf Recke
8 Hotel Kohlmayr
9 Goldener Hirsch
10 Pension Wolf
11 Hotel Tümmlerhof
12 Hotel Lärchenhof
13 Römischer Kaiser
14 Kaiserin Elisabeth
15 König von Ugarn

in Germany, Austria & Switzerland

Schloß Dürnstein

#1

A-3601 Dürnstein an der Donau
Austria
Telephone: 02711/212
Telex: 071 147
Singles 1010AS to 1130AS
Doubles 1560AS to 2200AS
Prices are half-board
Major cards.

Dürnstein, on the Danube in Austria's wine-producing Wachau Valley, about an hour's drive from Vienna, is one of the country's most picturesque villages. It is most appealing when approached by water. The *Donau* is especially lovely here and the stunning blue and white spire of the village church rises gracefully against the steep vineyards. High above the town is the ruined fortress where Richard the Lionhearted was held captive by his rival Leopold V, Duke of Austria, in the 12th century.

Schloß Dürnstein, once the summer residence of the Starhemberg Princes, is now a 37-room castle hotel. The building, constructed in 1630, sits in a favored position on a bluff overlooking the river. To enter the grounds, guests drive through an impressive arched entry into a graveled courtyard.

Inside, each of the public rooms — bar, library, restaurant — is handsomely decorated and furnished with fine rugs, paintings, antiques and *objets d'art*. White vaulted ceilings complete the sense of Old World elegance.

There is an outdoor terrace for dining and most tables enjoy splendid vistas of the Danube.

Our second floor corner room, Number 23, had three windows which looked out, not only on the river, but the vineyards, parts of the town and some of the fortress ramparts. It was large and comfortably furnished in a traditional style with an ancient dark wood ceiling with narrow beams, parquet floors and Oriental rugs. The bathroom was small and would not be comfortable for big people.

Some guest rooms are large and formal with crystal chandeliers, antique furnishings and porcelain stoves. First floor rooms open directly onto an elegant, wood-paneled drawing room with a grand piano.

Unfortunately, on a recent visit we found the food and, to a lesser extent, the service not up to the standard set by the hotel's physical attributes. Nonetheless, this is a wonderfully atmospheric hotel in a quiet, charming little wine village. You will enjoy your stay.

Hotel der Bär

#2

A-6352 Ellmau, Tirol
Austria
Telephone: 5358/2395
Telex: 051168
Fax: 05358/2395-56
Singles 950AS to 1250AS
Doubles 1900AS to 2400AS
Prices are half-board
No cards.

The **Hotel der Bär** in Ellmau, about an hour and a half's drive from Munich, below the Kaisergebirge range on the road between Kufstein and St. Johann, is spread over the side of a hill on several levels to take advantage of a fine view.

The warm welcome at this rambling resort is an attitude that continues throughout your stay. The Bär is one of those places where everybody from maid to manager smiles a *Grüss Gott* everytime there is eye contact.

The hotel is comfortable, unpretentious, and its public rooms have an open Tyrolean atmosphere that immediately puts guests at ease.

It has all the features of a five-star country resort, including two swimming pools, a beauty treatment center and supervised activities for children. There are tennis courts nearby, golf a few kilometers away in Kitzbühel, and, of course, plenty of hiking and skiing. But best of all, are the quiet mountain nights and fresh mountain mornings.

A good restaurant is especially important in a country hotel and the Bär's is better than good. In fact, the staff is so competent they make serving delicious food, in a comfortable, friendly atmosphere seem an effortless process, and that in itself is an art. The manager is likely to greet you by name and take you to your table. Lamps hanging over the big booths provide a cozy touch and from most tables there are excellent views. *Gault Millau* gives the cuisine two toques. We wouldn't argue.

Breakfast is from a giant buffet. In addition to the wide selection of the usual items, during our stay there were three kinds of scrambled eggs, sausage and fresh vegetables. If we were to rank the breakfasts served at the hotels in this book, the Bär's would be in the top five.

In the hotel's huge bar, a long wall of curving windows takes advantage of the view. There are acres, it seems, of couches and overstuffed chairs gathered around coffee tables. The layout is perfect for groups of 4 to 6 and makes for a wonderfully appealing room. After dinner it is a great place to settle in for coffee or a nightcap. One of the waitresses plays old records, usually American pop standards. A veritable stress-reduction clinic.

Austria

COUNTRY CASTLES

Two castles near Graz, both of which have recently been made into hotels, offer excellent accommodations in quiet, romantic settings. Both have restaurants, one of them outstanding, and both offer good value.

Schloß Obermayerhofen

#3

A-8272 Sebersdorf
Austria
Telephone: 03333/2503
Singles 400AS to 800AS
Doubles 800AS to 1600AS
Major cards.

Obermayerhofen, is located just off the Vienna-Graz autobahn about 50 kilometers east and a little north of Graz. On the Mair's map, *Die Generalkarte #5* for Österreich, you will see the notation in black lettering, 'Schl. Obermayerhofen,' just above the red letters for the off-ramp, 'Sebersdorf - Waltersdorf.'

The castle, once a stronghold against the Turks, in 1777 became the residence of the Counts of Kottulinsky. In 1985, the current Graf converted it to a hotel. A portion of the stable buildings became a restaurant, the **Hofstüberl**, and part became a gallerie where the Graf displays the works of local artists.

Its grounds, like so many schloß hotels of Europe, are not formally landscaped. One of the reasons the owners of these castles opted for the hotel business in the first place was because the property was too expensive to maintain as a private residence. Nonetheless, Obermayerhofen's grounds are green and lovely in a natural rather than a precisely groomed way. Automobile entry is from the road through an arch in one of the out-buildings and straight up a cobbled lane the couple of hundred yards to the castle's entrance. All around the three-story structure are wide lawns and deck chairs under the trees; perfect for an hour or two of reading.

We give Obermayerhofen high marks for romance, guest rooms and setting. Service was friendly but a little shaky. The economics of the business and the hotel's relatively remote location dictate a young, untrained staff. Sixteen-room hotels in the countryside are simply not able to hire graduates of the finest Swiss hotel schools.

Guest rooms are huge, high-ceilinged and comfortably furnished with antiques. Open your windows day or night and hear nothing but forest murmurs. Bathrooms are large and hospital-clean with 1990s fixtures. All rooms open to the inner courtyard. Our huge double, with a window opening onto the wooded grounds, was 1,300 schillings.

Dress is casual at the Hofstüberl. There are no more than a dozen tables and advance reservations are advised. The simple little room with its light wood wainscoting above a pale green banquette, and white ceiling intersected by dark wood beams, is cozy and informal. A four-course, fixed-price menu is about 400 schillings. The kitchen has a flair. Slices of tender rabbit liver sauteed with mint leaves and tiny red berries were delicious evidence of a creative chef. The restaurant is neither owned nor managed by the hotel, so do not expect to charge the bill to your room.

Schloß Plankenwarth

#4

A-8113 St. Oswald bei Graz
Austria
Telephone: 03123/2838
Singles 800AS to 1150AS
Doubles 1200AS to 1800AS
Major cards.

Use that same map — *Die Generalkarte* #5 for Österreich — to travel from Obermayerhofen over the the backroads west to **Schloß Plankenwarth**, about 15 kilometers west of Graz. (A pleasant detour is to go a little north and drive the Jogland Blumenstrasse in the Pöllauer Naturpark. At Obermayerhofen ask for the *Erlebnis Tour* brochure.)

For only three of its 900 years has Plankenwarth been a hotel. Once home for Styrian nobility and part of the chain of defense against the Turks, the castle was an SS headquarters during World War II and was purchased in 1981 by Graz attorney Gerhard Waisocher and his wife Friederike. The Waisochers have private quarters at the castle. In 1987, they added guest rooms and a restaurant.

Plankenwarth is more country and more relaxed than Obermayerhofen. It is also a more interesting structure and, while Obermayerhofen is prettily situated, Plankenwarth's location astride a wooded ridge is spectacular. The fortress is reached via a twisty, steep private road. There is guest parking in the courtyard.

Views in all directions are splendid. Look from the courtyard through the castle wall. The iron gate frames the terrace below and its inviting swimming pool nestled amid the trees. Beyond are the rolling green hills of Styria. A picture postcard view.

Guest rooms at the Plankenwarth are smaller than Obermayerhofen but more comfortably furnished and most have balconies, another advantage over Obermayerhofen. Both hotels, however, offer significant value. For about $100 double they provide country quiet in a romantic setting that fires the imagination. We stayed in the *Blaues*

Zimmer (1300 AS), one of seven double rooms. There are also four apartments suitable for more than two persons. The *Ostturm*, in one of the castle turrets, is especially attractive and rents for 2000 AS for four persons.

Like most of Plankenwarth's public areas, the breakfast room is special. It is on the castle's highest floor and its dark, rich, carved wood decor drops the time machine into full reverse gear. Tables for two are built into the deeply recessed windows of the castle's thick wall. At any of them you can enjoy the view through the trees across the green countryside, sip the morning's first cup of coffee and watch for the first sign of the advancing Turks — as someone surely must have done from that same spot hundreds of years ago.

Though it doesn't match the Obermayerhofen's outstanding food, Plankenwarth's restaurant serves plain, hearty fare at a good price in an attractive hunting lodge/knight's hall-style dining room.

Romantik Hotel Schwarzer Adler

#5

Kaiser Jägerstraße 2
A-6020 Innsbruck
Austria
Telephone: 05222/27109
Singles 450AS to 800AS
Doubles 1340AS to 2040AS
Major cards.

Thanks to its location along a major highway, its proximity to the Austrian Alps and its history as the host of two Winter Olympics, Innsbruck is well-visited by tour groups and their large, obnoxious busses. But while the package-trippers are led to their traps, you can enjoy what Innsbruck has to offer at the 28-room **Romantik Hotel Schwarzer Adler**.

Only a six or seven-minute walk from the center of town and a five-minute taxi ride from the train station, the Schwarzer Adler offers large rooms with fine views and good value.

Room Number 336 is decorated in traditional Tyrolean fashion. One of its two windows overlooks the pleasant garden two stories below, and there is a small sitting area with couch and chair, plus television, radio and writing table.

Public rooms are full of the usual touches: antiques, rich wood paneling and both vaulted and beamed ceilings. The welcome is friendly and, despite its location on a rather busy street, the hotel is quiet.

Schloß Haunsperg

The 50 Best Country Inns & Small, City Hotels

Schloß Haunsperg

#6

A-5411 Oberalm bei Hallein
Austria
Telephone: 6245/2662
Fax: 6245/5680
Singles 645AS
Doubles 1290AS to 1330AS
Suites 1560AS to 2160AS
Major cards.

If there is a prototypical Germany-Austria-Switzerland country hotel, **Schloß Haunsperg** may be it: just a handful of rooms in an old family house, the Alps surrounding quiet grounds; beautiful antique furniture everywhere, and, best of all, Erika and Georg von Gernerth, who treat their guests like honored family members.

The house (hotel seems too commercial a word) is at the edge of the tiny village of Oberalm bei Hallein, just 15 minutes south of Salzburg. It's easy to find, take the autobahn exit at Hallein, then head north toward Oberalm. A kilometer or two later you'll see a small sign indicating a right turn to Schloß Haunsperg, which is only another kilometer or so down this road. A word of warning: this road passes through the local industrial plant. Not the prettiest entry, but you'll never notice it once you are on the Haunsperg grounds.

Schloß Haunsperg was built in the 14th century and sits on a six-acre plot surrounded by tall trees and fields. Two six-story towers flank a four-story main house of stucco and stone; to the right is a Baroque chapel topped by a small bell tower. More about the chapel later.

In the house are just eight rooms; six suites and two doubles. There are usually no more than 16 guests and never more than 23. Rooms have telephones but no television or radio. Other than that, each of the accommodations is different in size, layout and furnishings.

The largest suite, called *Stern*, has two bedrooms plus a sitting room. The larger of the two bedrooms has two double beds with antique headboards inlaid with a star pattern. In the smaller room, which has only a twin bed, is a lady's chest of drawers built in 1736. The chest is in two sections: the top section of small drawers detaches from the rest of the piece so it can be used as a traveling case. And, since this was the 18th century, and an aristocratic lady had love letters and jewels to hide, the top section has several secret compartments. In the sitting room is a portrait of a beautiful young woman — a great-aunt of the family. The portrait is the only copy of a painting commissioned by Ludwig I, part of a collection of portraits of the most beautiful women of the world. The original is in the Residenz in Munich.

Also in this sitting room is a glass cabinet filled with porcelain figures, ivory fans, snuff boxes and other curios. What's most interesting about the cabinet is not its contents, but the fact that a case filled with valuable items is left unlocked. This trust is evident throughout Schloß Haunsperg. The von Gernerths are strongly committed to the idea that their home is just that — a home. Not a hotel, where guests are as faceless as their credit cards, and certainly not a museum. Herr and Frau von Gernerth *want* their guests to touch the furniture, to use the pieces as they were meant to be used. They truly want you to make yourself at home, to imagine what living in this castle was like hundreds of years ago.

The suite called *Zwischentrakt* is slightly smaller than the *Stern*, and occupies most of the small wing which links the chapel with the main house. The larger of the two bedrooms is built in what was the balcony in the chapel. When the chapel was in regular use, the balcony was used by the family to attend mass without having to mingle with the peasants. The floors in this suite are wide planks of light wood, contrasting with the dark tones of the two matching armoires and the mirrored dressing table. Another interesting piece in this room is a table with an inlaid wood representation of the *Hohensalzburg* castle.

Upstairs is a music room with a Bösendorfer grand piano. Music buffs may be interested to know that the young American conductor Andrew Lytton has played this instrument regularly over the years, first as a youth traveling with his parents (long-time regular guests of Schloß Haunsperg) and later when he lived at the house while he studied conducting in Salzburg. Lytton has gone on to become the youngest person to conduct at the Metropolitan Opera. Today the room is often used for chamber concerts.

The music room has several other interesting items, including a beautiful old bookcase with titles in several languages and a painting which shows the room's furnishings as they looked over one hundred years ago in their original setting in Vienna. The von Gernerths bought the entire room at auction and brought it back to Oberalm.

Two suites have entries to the music room. Book both and you may use the music room as your private salon, giving you virtually a whole floor as a private domain. And not all that expensive.

In the two doubles, *Arkaden* and *Kachelhofen*, are many fine antiques. One piece, in *Arkaden*, is an armoire built in 1354 as a wedding gift for a woman named Anna Moser.

Common areas are equally attractive. There are two breakfast rooms, one larger with a long, heavy wood table and antique sideboard, the other with a smaller, round table. In this second room is a portrait of Herr von Gernerth's great-grandfather, the lyricist for "The Blue Danube." A hand-written thank-you note from composer Johann Strauss hangs nearby.

The chapel attached to the hotel is a tiny church, dating from the late 14th century. The main attraction is the lovely altar which appears to be marble. However, the area around Hallein is so rich in marble, that when the altar was built, that stone was bypassed as being too common. Instead it was constructed of wood and then a *faux marbre* finish was applied by craftsmen. In the tabernacle is a rotating platform which turns to show three scenes, including a carved Mother and Child and a reliquary with a sliver of wood which is said to be from the actual cross of Christ.

In the chapel's belfry is a bell from 1570 — quite old, considering bells were usually melted down for weapons when wars came along and then recast as bells when peace reigned once more.

The welcome at Schloß Haunsperg is second to none. When guests arrive, one or both of the proprietors will greet them, help get luggage upstairs and then extend an invitation to share a glass of wine. Breakfast (the only meal served) is at no set time. If you want to sleep 'til noon and then eat, that's fine. Or, if you must be on the road early and want breakfast at six a.m., that's OK, too. Again, when you leave, one or both of the von Gernerths will be on hand to bid you farewell.

In summer you can sit in the garden or play tennis on the private court. The von Gernerths also love planning sightseeing tours for their guests, or making dinner reservations or finding a baby sitter for the children.

Jagdschloß Graf Recke

#7

A-5742 Wald im Pinzgau
Austria
Telephone: 06565/6417
Telex: 66711
Singles 350AS to 480AS
Doubles 980AS to 1260AS
Visa, Diners Club.

You are driving east through Austria, down the mountain road from the Gerlos Pass in the Kitzbüheler Alpen region. You have just seen the spectacular Krimml falls, the highest in Europe. At the village of Wald im Pinzgau is the small sign you've been searching for. A left turn takes you a quarter of a mile along a narrow, gravel road. Across a meadow is your destination, the **Jagdschloß Graf Recke**, an authentic hunting lodge operated by the Count and Countess von der Recke. The Graf himself may descend the front steps to greet you.

His lodge was built in 1925 by the late Gottard Count von der Recke who came from Silesia (now part of Poland) to hunt. The family once held the shooting rights to what is now a national park, the vast *Hohen Tauern*. In 1953, the lodge was enlarged and converted to a hotel. Today it is a charming reminder of an almost extinct way of life. This is not a hotel of great luxury, but one of some comfort, in a magnificent physical setting, marinating in atmosphere.

Public rooms have a museum quality, with dozens of mounted horns, stuffed trophies, porcelain from Meissen and Berlin, as well as other treasures. In the lounge, where in the old days the men would repair for port and cigars, the walls are crowded with horns — mostly chamois and deer — and there is a carved family armoire topped by a giant stuffed bird.

Guest rooms are spacious and comfortable. Each has a separate sitting area and a porcelain stove to ward off the chill of winter. There are interesting prints on the walls, and wonderful views from the balconies. The front terrace — off the breakfast room and partially shaded by a large pine tree — has a view across the meadow to the mountains and is the place for breakfast, lunch and snacks on good weather days. There is an outdoor swimming pool in a secluded garden and the hotel is minutes from dozens of ski lifts. A 45-kilometer cross-country ski trail passes the Jagdschloß.

Graf Recke is a gracious host, eager to share the stories and legends of his family with visitors. He can usually obtain tickets for his guests to summer music events in Salzburg and can also arrange for transportation as well as facilities for dressing and dining at a castle hotel in Salzburg, approximately 100 miles away.

The Graf can also suggest a number of easy mountain walks which he says are intended more for promenaders than alpinists. He has prepared a simple printed guide with precise directions for seven separate days of walking around the Oberpinzgau. There are special activities at Christmas and the Graf recommends the holidays as the best time to visit.

For those who seek luxury accommodations, the Jagdschloß Graf Recke may seem a bit too rustic. Many, though, will find it — as we did — a relaxing country hideaway. And, with its location in the *Hohen Tauern* National Park, there is much to see and do.

Hotel Kohlmayr

#8

A-5562 Obertauern
Austria
Telephone: 06456/272282
Per person rates 450AS to 1500AS
Major cards.

Life is slow in the tiny Austrian village of Obertauern. From late fall to late spring, skiers ply the slopes above this town which lies at the top of the old Roman road which separates the Austrian states of Salzburg and Carthinia. In summer, a few hikers come to explore the mountains. The only other reason to visit here is the **Hotel Kohlmayr**, easily among the best "ski hotels" anywhere.

It is certainly the best-equipped we've seen. The Kohlmayr has everything you'd expect — friendly staff, comfortable rooms, pool, saunas, Jacuzzi, a separate skier's entry — plus some things you wouldn't expect.

Rooms are clean and simply-decorated. Baths tend to be on the small side, but the beds are quite comfortable and all rooms have TV and radio. Many have small sitting areas. But it is the common areas which set the Kohlmayr apart from the competition. The main bar is an excellent example: a carved wood bar guards one side of the room, which is beautifully decorated in pastels and features a lovely chevron-patterned light wood floor. There is a fine view of the surrounding mountains. It is an inviting place to have a drink after a hard day—or even an easy one.

Downstairs is a large indoor pool, Jacuzzi and two saunas. The intelligence that went into the design of this near-perfect skier's inn is embodied in a door which leads to an enclosed area where one can — after sweating in the sauna — roll naked in the snow, unseen by passers-by. Of course, you may pass on this activity, but there are those who relish such things and allowances have been made for them.

Our favorite part of the Hotel Kohlmayr is a music room, the like of which we have seen in no other hotel. Here you can relax in one of several comfortable leather chairs, put your feet up, don a pair of high-quality headphones, place a compact disc from Herr Kohlmayr's collection in a player located in a small cabinet at your side and enjoy the music. There are also loudspeakers and a game table so a group of friends can listen and play cards.

Though there is little to do in Obertauern other than athletic endeavors, the comforting, relaxing atmosphere of the Kohlmayr would make a wonderful refuge for non-skiers, too. And if culture tempts you, Salzburg is less than an hour away when the weather is good. (If the weather is bad, driving may not be the best idea — take the shuttle bus to Radstadt and continue on the train to Salzburg.)

… Austria …

SALZBURG

Salzburg is known as Mozart's city. In his time, though, the city was not terribly fond of Mozart or his music and he returned the favor. Writing to his father, Mozart spoke often of the city of his birth. *"I have no pleasures here,"* he wrote from Vienna, *"save the single one of being away from Salzburg!"*

Walking through today's Salzburg, one would never realize that at one time Mozart was not the biggest thing since sliced *brot*. Everywhere you turn, the name or likeness of the famed composer greets you. The Mozartplatz. The Mozart Cinema. One almost expects to find Don Giovanni Dry Goods or Cosi fan Tutte Cleaners.

Still, Salzburg is a marvelous town, and the best way to experience it is to stay in the *altstadt* where everything is within walking distance.

Hotel Goldener Hirsch

#9

Getreidegasse 37
A-5020 Salzburg
Austria
Telephone: 0662/848511
Telex: 632967
Singles 1800AS to 2400AS
Doubles 2950AS to 4500AS
Major cards.

The **Hotel Goldener Hirsch** is Salzburg's best hotel and *the* place to stay during the city's famous summer music festival.

Despite its location on the busy pedestrian-only Getreidegasse, it is a sanctuary from the bustle of the old town. Its 75 rooms are decorated in the most tasteful implementation of Salzburger style we've seen, and the lobby, restaurant and breakfast room are warm and inviting. The color scheme of loden green and grey is used throughout the hotel — but without sacrificing each room's individual charm.

The service, like the decor, is understated excellence. The staff always seems present at the right time, yet with no sense of hovering and awaiting the snap of your fingers. They do not seem stuffy or arrogant. On the contrary, they do everything they can to make you feel like an important guest.

Austria

Gartenhotel Tümmlerhof

#11

A-6100 Seefeld/Tirol
Austria
Telephone: 05212/2571-0
Telex: 3522350
Singles 850AS to 1630AS
Doubles 1480AS to 3260AS
Prices are half-board
No cards.

    The **Gartenhotel Tümmlerhof** is about 1200 meters north of the village on the west side of Münchner Straße. It's location on four wooded acres combines country charm with easy access to Seefeld's busy pedestrian-only shopping areas.

    We found the hotel so appealing we stayed an extra night for one of the most pleasant dining experiences of a long trip. Each Wednesday, the Tümmlerhof hosts an outdoor (weather permitting) barbecue. Tables and umbrellas are set on the terrace and lawn, the staff dresses in traditional Tyrolean costume and a great ice carving is centerpiece for a massive layout of food that looks wonderful and tastes even better. Several white-toqued chefs barbecue and serve an array of delicious meats including various wursts, chops, steaks and fowl. Members of the handsome Zorn family, the Tümmlerhof's owners, graciously greet arrivals and serve them from the buffet, all the while urging extra helpings onto plates already top-heavy with food. Throw in live music from the venerable string trio and, of course, magnificent views of the mountains, and you have a most agreeable package. Best of all, the barbecue is included in the half board arrangement for hotel guests, as is the Friday night five-course degustation menu. (Note the Tümmlerhof's kitchen gets two red toques and four red knives and forks from *Gault Millau*, thereby placing it — by *Gault Millau* standards, anyway — among Austria's top ten restaurants.)

    From the road, the Tümmlerhof is nothing special. Even inside at the reception desk, the hotel seems plain. But once into the clubby atmosphere of its public salons and restaurants, the mood changes to a sense of understated affluence. Not stiff or formal but an environment of relaxed comfort and unobtrusive service.

The hotel's 65 rooms are spacious, well furnished and designed for long stays. Nearly all have entry closets with plenty of shelves, places to hang clothing and to store gear. Room Number 325 is most pleasant with a balcony and view over the hotel garden toward the village. We paid 1760 AS per night, an off-season rate which included breakfast and dinner. Number 325 is in the hotel's category of slightly larger rooms. These offer several advantages over the regular doubles and singles: they are south facing, have balconies, better furnishings and the toilet and shower/bath are in separate rooms. The difference in price is about 200 AS per person.

We also inspected Number 422, one of the smaller doubles. It was comfortable, had a sloping beam ceiling and an ample bathroom but no balcony and overlooked the parking lot.

In winter, guests can take advantage of the hotel's proximity to intermediate and beginning ski areas. One is within walking distance and a free bus runs on the half hour to the other.

The Tümmlerhof has all the services of a resort hotel. There are bikes which guests can borrow at no charge, though the two we used were in need of repair. There is even free child care for a few hours each day in the well equipped game room.

The hotel's lovely, park-like grounds, quiet location, range of services and excellent kitchen make it an ideal choice for families.

Hotel Lärchenhof

#12

A-6100 Seefeld/Tirol
Austria
Telephone: 05212/2383
Telex: 533962
Singles 600AS to 790AS
Doubles 1360AS to 3240AS
Prices are half-board
American Express, Diners Club.

The most physically attractive of these two Seefeld hotels is the **Lärchenhof**. This 50-room gem is set in the trees on a small hill overlooking the town. On summer mornings, some two dozen identical chaise lounges are pointed precisely south, in readiness for the arrival of sun-seeking guests. A striped, yellow towel is folded and placed at exactly the same spot on each chaise. Such precision is evident throughout the hotel.

Some of the Lärchenhof's public areas rival anything we have seen in a small hotel. In the tremendously inviting little bar just off the entry, you not only see the wood of the beautifully carved ceiling and walls, but smell it as well. One of the coziest rooms you'll find in a country whose speciality is cozy.

Pass through the glass door marked *Aquarena* to the hotel's elegant spa. A shallow marble pool is surrounded by mirrored pillars. Its ornate gold fixtures expel quiet streams of water. Everything — walls, floors, fountain — is marble. The ceiling is a circular, stained glass skylight. This is the main grotto. Off it, through other clear glass doors, are grottos for steam bath, sauna, solarium, cold pool immersion, and so on. It is absolutely Roman. In the '50s and '60s, the Lärchenhof's Aquarena would have been a money-making tourist attraction for most American small towns.

There is a sparkling indoor pool which opens onto the garden and provides a view down the hill toward the village.

The cellar bar, paneled in dark, rich wood, has a small marble dance floor.

Big, comfortable guest rooms almost match the public rooms in Tyrolean opulence. Entry doors are surrounded with heavy wood frames and lintels. Room numbers are lighted.

The south-facing rooms are the more desirable and Number 217 is a double in this category. It is finished in dark wood, dark beams and white, rough plaster walls. There is a shared balcony. From the table built into the curving windows is a wonderful 90 degree view of the region.

The bathroom has separate toilet and shower and a bidet. The fixtures and towels are a bright yellow against the shiny brown floor-to-ceiling tile.

The less expensive north-facing rooms do not have sitting areas, but are the same in all other respects except price.

If the larger, more rambling Tümmlerhof is the place for families, the elegant, more secluded Lärchenhof is for couples.

Its kitchen, however, is not as distinguished as the Tümmlerhof.

To reach the hotel, go north on Münchner Straße from the center of town and turn left on Geigenbühel Straße. Look for the Hotel Larchenhof signs, take the right hand driveway and go down into the parking lot.

VIENNA

That first-time glimpse of a great city, like Christmas morning and settling behind the wheel of a new car, is guaranteed to race the pulse and fire the imagination. Even travelers with the romantic soul of a mortgage banker will flatten their noses against an airplane window for a first look at the Eiffel Tower or the New York skyline.

Such behavior on the 20th visit to a city, however, means the traveler is either an emotional adolescent or the city is indeed one of the world's greatest. In the case of your authors and Vienna, both are true. Forgetting sentimentality, even the most sophisticated and jaded traveler would have to place Vienna near the top of any list of great cities.

Musically, it has no peer. Its orchestras and opera companies, as well as their several venues, are the world's finest. Graves in the city's *Zentral Friedhof* bear testimony to the city's musical preeminence. Buried there — among others — are Brahms, Beethoven, Schubert, the Strausses and Franz von Suppe. All produced many of their greatest works here. And, of course, this is the city of Mozart, the one he loved far more than his home town of Salzburg.

In the German-speaking world, Vienna stands behind only Berlin as a theatrical center.

Someone else can calculate which city has the most Rembrandts, Holbeins, Raphaels, Bruegels, Reubens and Dürers, but there are more than enough for even the pickiest art patron at the Albertina, the *Kunsthistorisches* Museum and the Upper Belvedere.

Then there are the lesser — but no less lively — arts, such as the coffee houses, the *Heurigen*, the *Prater*, Viennese pastry (but pass on the *Sachertorte* — overrated) and the highest-brow street music anywhere.

If you haven't been, you must go. Of, course, if you have, you know you must go again.

Hotel Römischer Kaiser

The 50 Best Country Inns & Small, City Hotels

# Römischer Kaiser

#13

Annagasse 6
A-1010 Vienna
Austria
Telephone: 0222/51227510
Telex: 113696.
Singles 1200AS
Doubles 1540AS to 1990AS
Major cards.

A sparkling little jewel of a hotel on the narrow, pedestrian-only Annagasse, about 200 meters off the Kärntnerstraße is the 27-room **Römischer Kaiser**. Price aside, this is our first choice among the small hotels of Vienna. The Römischer Kaiser typifies all that is good in small European city hotels. It is well located, no more than a few minutes' walk from the major Ring sights, impeccably run and utterly charming.

Much of the charm comes from its owner, Dr. Gerhard Jungreuthmayer, who resembles a younger, better-looking brother to the Swiss actor, Maximilian Schell.

The hotel was once a small, private palace. It is more than 300 years old and, because of that and its baroque architecture, is protected by a national trust. In 1907, the current owner's grandfather converted the building to a hotel.

Entering from the Annagasse side (there is another entrance from Krugerstraße) guests are immediately struck by the small but exquisitely decorated public rooms: crystal chandeliers, Oriental rugs, period furniture and dark wood. The vaulted ceilings, pillars and walls are painted in the traditional white and yellow of the baroque style.

Rooms are elegantly decorated and have nearly every amenity, including Dr. Jungreuthmayer's latest pride and joy, small safes in each room which can be programmed in less than a minute to be opened only by the magnetic strip on the back of your major credit card.

Number 6 is a small double but the only one in the house which retains the original 300-year old ceiling, painted in white with gold trim. Numbers 12 and 30, both on the inner courtyard, are the hotel's largest. Each has three beds. We also recommend Number 26, with large bath and two windows opening on the usually quiet Annagasse.

The hotel staff can arrange opera and theatre tickets (20% over face value, standard ticket agency commission in Vienna) or pick up guests at the airport. If you order opera tickets from the U.S. at the regular price through the Staatsoper ticket office and receive the confirmation card, you may — provided you have reservations at the Römischer Kaiser — send the card (no money) to the hotel. The hotel will pick up the tickets, pay for them and hold them until your arrival. A convenience because tickets must be picked up and paid for at the box office at least 48 hours prior to performances.

There is a breed of independent European hoteliers — Claas Johannsen at the **Benen Diken Hof** on the German island of Sylt immediately comes to mind — who, through a special combination of intelligence, taste, commitment and personal charm, are able to create a truly *gemütlich* hotel. Running a small hotel in Europe is a fiercely competitive, demanding business. There are literally thousands of fine little hotels in Germany, Austria and Switzerland. Few, however, achieve what Dr. Jungreuthmayer has with the Römischer Kaiser. Believe him when he says, "We stay close to our clients, we have time for our guests."

Reservations at the Römischer Kaiser must be made well in advance, though it can't hurt to try on short notice for there are occasional cancellations.

Parking inside the Ring is difficult. The hotel has arranged for guest parking at the nearby Beethoven garage for a daily charge of about 200AS.

Austria

Paulusstuben. 1st district, Walfischgasse 7, telephone 512 81 36. A little touristy but plenty of Old World atmosphere and decent live music. Moderate.

Stadtbeisl. 1st district, Naglergasse 21, telephone 533 33 23. Others listed here are better but the welcome is friendly and the food o.k. Inexpensive.

WE DO NOT RECOMMEND:

Griechenbeisl. 1st district, Fleischmarkt 11, telephone 533 19 77. Live zither or accordion music and pleasant atmosphere in one of the oldest, busiest restaurants in Vienna. We keep trying this place but the food just doesn't make it. Moderate.

Mathiaskeller. 1st district, Maysedergasse 2, telephone 512 21 67. Caters to tourists, large groups. Sometimes rude service. Spirtless Gypsy music. Moderate.

OFF THE WALL:

Heurigen Restaurant. 3rd district, 47 Rennweg. Only for the adventurous. Working class clientele. Forget the food, go listen to the tenor voice and accordion of Walter Meda who knows all the *Wien lieder*—the songs every Viennaphile wants to hear. Good Budweiser *vom fass*. Not for the timid. Little English spoken.

Germany

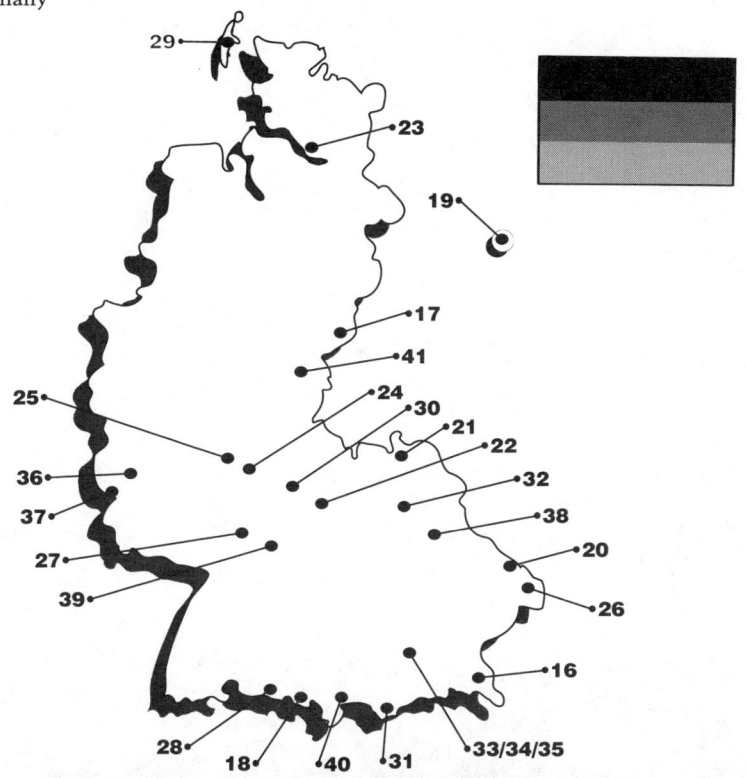

GERMANY

16 Hotel Hofwirt
17 Harzhotel Romantischer Winkel
18 Strand-Hotel Tannhof
19 Hotel Am Zoo
20 Hotel Andrea
21 Hotel Blankenburg
22 Waldhotel Polisina
23 Hotel Abtei
24 Hotel Birkenhof
25 Hotel Sonnenhof
26 Romantik Hotel Bierhütte
27 Hotel Hirschgasse
28 Villa Bellevue
29 Hotel Benen Diken-Hof
30 Hotel Anker
31 Berghotel Latscheneck
32 Hotel Feiler
33 Hotel Prinzregent
34 Hotel Exquisit
35 Hotel An der Oper
36 Gutshotel des Weingutes
37 Petrisberg
38 Weinhaus Steichele
39 Schoßhotel Friedrichruhe
40 Hotel Bavaria
41 Schloß Hotel Spangenberg

in Germany, Austria & Switzerland

Hotel Hofwirt

#16

Salzburger Straße 21
D-8230 Bad Reichenhall
West Germany
Telephone: 08651/62021
Singles: 70DM to 90DM
Doubles: 100DM to 120DM
No cards.

Like Salzburg, its Austrian neighbor, Bad Reichenhall achieved its wealth and status through the salt trade. Salt mining continues today — why change something that's been going on for 2400 years — but the town's major attractions now are the spas which are among the finest in Europe and reputed to be especially helpful for those with respiratory problems.

Bad Reichenhall is beautifully situated, the Bavarian Alps rising at the edge of town provide a diversion for walkers and protection from chilling winds. Parks and other green spaces abound. There is even a casino for those searching for more exciting pursuits than mountain walks, reading and spa treatments.

The town is primarily hotels, so you have a wide variety of lodging choices. The best small hotel is the 20-room **Hotel Hofwirt**, located in the quietest section of town, directly across from *Karlspark*, the town's largest park. It is also convenient to the many *wanderwegs*, or footpaths, leading into the nearby mountains. It also has one of the better restaurants in town.

Originally built in 1835, the Hofwirt was completely remodeled four years ago — though the hotel is so well-maintained the remodeling could have been done just four *months* ago. The exterior is stucco and painted an attractive peach color. Inside, the lobby and restaurant are decorated in light woods; vaulted ceilings of white plaster give the common areas a sense of formality.

Rooms are relatively large, most offer views of the park and mountains, and the beds have thick down comforters. There is also an attractive beer garden, a perfect place to relax on a warm summer evening after a long walk.

The restaurant is excellent and offers good value. We were especially impressed by the *rehgoulasch* (venison goulash) with mushrooms and cranberries, served with some of the best homemade *spätzle* we have encountered. In fact, if the dish you order at the Hofwirt comes with *spätzle*, you can't go far wrong. Dinner for two, without wine, will be around 60DM to 100DM — a bargain.

Breakfast, taken in the same room, is also a treat, with a large selection of fresh juices, meats, cheeses and breads.

Harzhotel Romantischer Winkel

#17

Bismarckstraße 23
D-3423 Bad Sachsa
West Germany
Telephone: 05523/1005
Singles 76DM to 105DM
Doubles 118DM to 148DM
American Express, Mastercard.

Not many people pass through the Harz mountain town of Bad Sachsa. Located 129 kilometers southeast of Hannover in a bubble of land that curves into East Germany, most roads don't go much beyond this quiet spa town of 5000 inhabitants.

Even fewer Americans make it to Bad Sachsa, though the reception that awaits them at the **Harzhotel Romantischer Winkel** would certainly bring them back once they found their way. Only a handful of the staff speak English, and none to whom we spoke were fluent; but all are so friendly and eager you will not find it a problem.

The hotel's *gemütlich* atmosphere is evident the moment you walk through the door. It's difficult to describe, but the Romantischer Winkel is the kind of place where you feel like a regular on your first visit.

The Romantischer Winkel has recently been remodeled and the decorator cut no corners. There is rich mahogany, fine wallpaper and comfortable furnishings. The 42 rooms are spotless. There is also an indoor swimming pool, sauna and solarium.

Bad Sachsa is a quiet town, one with little automobile traffic, surrounded by forests, seemingly undisturbed by a world outside. It has that ambience that seems to be present only in towns located where the road ends. Iseltwald, in Switzerland (home of the **Chalet du Lac**, also included in this book) has the same feeling. Bad Sachsa is the type of place to which one sends tense executives who refuse to relax unless forced to; and when they arrive, they realize relaxing is what they'd been wanting to do all along.

The comfort and welcome of this establishment would be enough to merit inclusion in this volume. Add to this a fine restaurant and the package is complete. We have eaten at the Romantischer Winkel on three separate occasions, and in all instances the food was excellent and the portions more than generous. The service, as it is at the hotel, is top-notch.

A HARZ MOUNTAIN DRIVE

While most travelers prefer the cities and countryside of southern Germany, the north has its own brand of charm, some of which you will see on this drive through the *Solling/Vogler* National Park and into the Harz Mountains. For it you will need *Die Generalkarte* map # 9, available in Germany at many bookstores and most Shell stations.

The drive begins in the town of Beverungen. Leave town on Red Road 241 (the color on the map), cross the river Weser and head west through a forest of deciduous trees. Turn left on Red Road 497, following the signs toward Neuhaus and Holzminden. As you near the village of Neuhaus, the forest's character will slowly change from mostly deciduous to mostly evergreen trees.

At the edge of Neuhaus is a small *wildpark* where one can walk along a path and view animals such as boar and reindeer in a natural setting. There is also a small restaurant, the **Restaurant am Wildpark**, which serves plain German cuisine in relatively large quantities. Though the food is nothing special, the chef is at least concerned that you enjoy your meal. When one of our party was unable to clean his plate, the chef came out of the kitchen, a look of genuine concern on his face, and asked if the food was not to our liking and would we care for something else — on the house, of course.

Leave Neuhaus via the Yellow Road leading to Dassel and Einbeck. Just before Dassel will be a long, straight descent into the Leine river valley, a flat plain some 20 kilometers wide, criss-crossed by many feeder streams. At Einbeck, turn north on Red Road 3. Approximately four kilometers later, head east again on Red Road 64 toward Seesen and the Hannover autobahn.

Near the town of Greene you will drive under an old railroad trestle, perhaps 100 feet high and built in the style of a Roman aqueduct. Between Greene and Bad Gandersheim the countryside shows the effects of industrialization and is not very attractive. However, it is along this stretch of road that you will get your first view of the Harz mountains. After crossing under the autobahn, turn left toward Seesen. In Seesen, watch for the sign pointing to *Schildautalklinik*, approximately two blocks beyond the turn to Red Road 242.

The Harz stand as the first obstacle to the winds and storms blowing in off the Baltic and therefore receive quite a bit of rain and snow; you might find this drive a bit tricky during the winter months.

As you climb up this Yellow Road, past the handsome buildings of the *Talklinik*, the woods become dark and deep, the trees tightly packed; it is not difficult to imagine trolls and other creatures of Germanic legends occupying these mysterious forests.

Approximately one kilometer past the summit you will turn right on a Red Road heading toward Clausthal-Zellerfeld. At the village of Lautenthal, notice the large, operating mill wheel at the mine here. Tours in English are available. Mining, incidentally, is one of the major industries of the Harz mountains and you may be disturbed by the scars this trade has left on the landscape. The areas which have been left untouched, however, are quite lovely.

Past the touristy enclave of Wildemann, go east on Red Road 242 toward Clausthal-Zellerfeld and Braunlage. At the intersection of Red Roads 242 and 4, turn left toward Bad Harzburg, driving through beautiful forests and past the waterfall at Radau. Your scenic drive is officially ended when you see the Hotel Schmeltzer in Bad Harzburg, a monstrosity in green that is our nomination for ugliest hotel in Germany.

An alternate end to this journey is to turn right on Red Road 4 and continue to Bad Sachsa and the **Romantischer Winkel**.

Strand-Hotel Tannhof

#18

Oeschländer Weg 24
8990 Schachen
West Germany
Telephone: 08382/6044
Singles 79DM to 135DM
Doubles 146DM to 259DM
No cards.

 The moment you turn the car down the long drive and begin rolling through the lovely grounds of the **Strand-Hotel Tannhof**, it is clear you are about to experience a fine hotel. Ahead, across the lawn and down a slope that ends at the shore of the Bodensee, partially hidden among stately old trees, is the century-old, three-story *Schlößchen* — the hotel's main building. Just to the right of the entrance is a more modern guest house whose principal advantages are balcony views of the park and handsome main building. At the rear of the *schlößchen*, an inviting terrace overlooks the hotel's private beach, the lake and the old town of Lindau on its small, flat island.

 The high ceilings, hardwood floors and graceful furnishings give the public rooms of the main building a feeling of traditional elegance. Not chic — but well-worn, easy and comfortable. Guest rooms provide immaculate comfort in spacious surroundings with all amenities. There are just 29 rooms in the hotel.

 Breakfast at the Tannhof is from the buffet and replete with the usual German *frühstück* goodies: the freshest breads, cheeses, butter and sliced meats. From the guest house it is a short walk to the main building for meals, hardly an inconvenience since the journey is through the park-like grounds.

 In season, Lindau attracts hordes of tourists who crowd its narrow streets and walkways. The Strand-Hotel Tannhof, in quiet Schachen — perhaps three kilometers from Lindau's *zentrum* — offers a placid retreat from such hubbub. The hotel is closed from October to mid-March.

BERLIN

Great cities evoke emotions. In Vienna it's a romantic dreaminess inspired by Lehar and Strauss melodies and the ghosts of Beethoven and Mozart. Paris is the European traveler's Disneyland: everything looks so good, tastes so good and feels so good one doesn't know quite where to begin.

What one comes to feel about Berlin is more visceral and complex. This unique city can uncover several emotions — anger, pride, frustration — which one doesn't commonly experience in other European cities. Perhaps it's Berlin's recent history that sets it apart.

In the '20s Berlin may have been the world's intellectual core. Vladimir Nabokov wrote here, Vladimir Horowitz played here and Albert Einstein thought here. Competing Berlin orchestras were conducted by Otto Klemperer, Bruno Walter and Wilhelm Furtwängler. The films of Ernst Lubitsch and Fritz Lang featured Greta Garbo, Marlene Dietrich and Peter Lorre. Some think that had it not been for WWII, Berlin would still be the world's film capital. Berlin theater marquees bore the names of Kurt Weill, Lotte Lenya, Bertolt Brecht and Max Reinhardt. The impact of Walter Gropius' Bauhaus school of architecture over the past 60 years cannot be measured.

The Berlin of the Cold War has been divided and distributed among the Allies and there are now two cities, East and West. It is probably this Berlin that most stirs the blood. The contrast between one — a lovely place of lakes, forests, gardens, farms and a pulsating urban center, all made an island by a heavily fortified encircling wall — and the lifeless, gray other, presents an accessible and tangible demonstration of the ideological differences between NATO countries and those of the Warsaw Pact.

The best Cold War archive and repository of Wall paraphernalia is the scruffy but riveting little museum, **Haus am Checkpoint Charlie** at 44 Friedrichstraße. Here are displayed the remnants of more than 25 years of escapes and escape attempts through, over and under that detestable structure.

Berlin is an amazing city, unlike any other in the world. It is not to be missed.

Hotel Am Zoo

#19

Kurfürstendamm 25
1000 Berlin 15
West Germany
Telephone: 030/883091
Singles 120DM to 150DM
Doubles 190DM to 215DM
Major cards.

The small hotel in Berlin which best combines the virtues of location, comfort and value is the **Hotel Am Zoo**. Though larger (145 rooms) than what we usually consider a small city hotel, we have included it because it stands well above the other offerings in the city. On the Kurfürstendamm, only a block from the stylish but pricey Kempinski-Bristol, it's as near as a good hotel gets to the center of Berlin action. Virtually everything in the way of restaurants and shopping at the city center is within a short stroll.

The Am Zoo, built in 1891, is a lovingly restored old hotel which offers the advantages of large rooms and high ceilings along with modern amenities. The decorative emphasis, both in the common areas and guest rooms, is polished dark wood. The appealing entry and lobby, open to the mezzanine, is decorated with rich paneling, brass trim and modern light fixtures.

Most rooms have 14-foot ceilings, color TV, radio, large tiled baths and floor space enough for a sitting area with couch and comfortable chairs. The windows of rooms in the inner section open onto a courtyard — making for quiet nights in this noisy city. In the morning, though, you may be awakened by the raucous call of peacocks, presumably from Berlin's famous Zoological Park a few blocks away.

Large rooms in big city hotels don't come cheap, but the Am Zoo's rates are remarkably moderate. Double rooms run from 190DM to 215DM, and we can't think of a heart-of-the-big-city hotel that's a better bargain. Parking is free for guests — an important consideration in crowded downtown Berlin.

A SHORT STROLL TO A GOOD RESTAURANT

The sign outside says *Estiatorio*, the Greek word for bistro, but the place is known as **Fofi**, for the exotic-looking woman who runs this Berlin version of all the smart, bistro-style restaurants you've ever seen, from San Francisco's Washington Square Bar & Grill to Café de la Paix in Paris. The clientele is a mix of jet-setters, media types, down-at-the-heel artists, plus friends of the great and near-great who frequent such spots. Terrific people watching.

It is said by those who should know that Fofi's was background for a scene from John le Carré's Little Drummer Girl. In the book, Gadi Becker "hastened to a fashionable Greek nightclub he knew of, run by a woman of cosmopolitan wisdom." Fofi is the wise woman and if you've read the book you know Becker had a good time.

Fofi's walls are covered with an eclectic mélange of art from scrap wood sculptures (notice the Egyptian woman with the two-piece bathing suit) to contemporary paintings. White linens, creaky plank flooring repaired in spots with strips of tin, rough brass light fixtures and waiters in shirts, ties and belt-to-ankle starched white aprons fit the bistro style perfectly. The menu is a la carte and reasonably priced. The cuisine, which leans toward the Adriatic, is simple and delicious with numerous lamb entrees and lots of seafood. A good start to a meal is a combination of the best of the restaurant's hot and cold *vorspeisen*. The superb *dolmas* highlight this small plate of exotic tastes. Among entrees, the scampi, in a sauce which one chooses from among three, is faultless. *Moussaka* is a good pick if you fancy eggplant, and the several lamb dishes are house specialities. Dinner for two, including wine, espresso and dessert will range from DM100 to DM150.

Though service is friendly and competent, please realize you might not be attended to in quite the same manner as regular customers, the ones Fofi hugs and kisses.

Reservations at Fofi are not difficult early in the evening, but you may want to try for a table after 8 p.m. when the regulars begin to arrive and the pace starts to quicken.

Fofi's Estiatorio, Fasanenstraße 70, 1000 Berlin 15, telephone (030) 8 81 87 85. No cards.

Hotel Andrea

#20

Hölzlweg 10
D-8373 Bodenmais
West Germany
Telephone: 09924/386
Singles 69DM to 94DM
Doubles 138DM to 158DM
Prices are half-board
Mastercard.

The **Hotel Andrea**, in the Bavarian Forest in the quiet town of Bodenmais, is the kind of place that makes one feel very far away from things like rush-hour traffic jams and skies brown with pollution.

The Andrea is a perfect spot to spend a week away from the world's cares, your needs attended to by Herr Eichner, the proprietor, who is ever-present, ever-cordial and dressed always in traditional Bavarian lodenwear. The Eichner family extends as warm a welcome as we have found in a country which prides itself on such things. One is met with a broad smile, a handshake and immediately relieved of luggage.

On lovely grounds overlooking the old section of Bodenmais, the hotel has a secluded garden for reading or sunbathing and a small covered terrace perfectly suited for snacks or just for gazing out over the valley. Inside, all is paneled and Bavarian, with heavy furniture and thick rugs. The 26 rooms are large and lovingly-maintained. Number 18, on the ground floor, is full of light and air with blond furniture and a beautifully tiled bathroom.

Accommodations at the Andrea include breakfast and dinner. Service in the dining room is friendly and informal, though at dinner, women will probably feel more comfortable in a dress, men in a jacket. Breakfast is from a tempting and ample buffet. At dinner there is a choice of three or four entrees. The cuisine, while attractively presented, is not distinguished. Afterward, adjourn to the cozy, wood-paneled bar for a drink, a game of cards or conversation.

One needn't reach for the wallet each time a drink or snack is served here; transactions are quietly noted and appear on the final bill.

Hotel Blankenburg

#21

Rosenauer Straße 30
D-4590 Coburg
West Germany
Telephone: 09561/75005
Singles 75DM to 105DM
Doubles 115DM to 215DM
Major cards.

Though surrounded on three sides by East Germany, and located farther north than Frankfurt, the little town of Coburg has been part of Bavaria since 1920. But with the grapes of Franken wines growing only a few kilometers away, and the massive Veste — known as the "Franconian Crown" — overlooking the town, that can only be the result of a gerrymander. The town seems far more Franconian than Bavarian.

Once an important stop on the road to Berlin, Dresden and other points east, Coburg is now a peaceful village attractive for its historic significance and to those wishing to tour the nearby Hümmel factory in Rödental or to drive north to the forbidding East German border crossing.

The major attraction of Coburg is the Veste, a fortress which hovers above the town, fading in and out of the clouds. Martin Luther holed up in this triple-walled citadel for five months in 1530, awaiting his day before the Augsburg Imperial Diet. You can tour his apartment. There is also an art collection of some note which includes paintings by Rembrandt and Albrecht Dürer. There are antique wedding carriages, an extraordinary display of armour and weapons — the largest in Germany — and a cabinet displaying some 20,000 coins and medals,

Downtown on the Schloßplatz is Ehrenburg Castle, where it is claimed, Europe's first flush toilet was unveiled. Ehrenburg was the boyhood home of Prince Albert, whose likeness is found not only on millions of tobacco cans around the world, there is a statue of him in Coburg's marketplace.

Coburg is also home to an excellent little country inn, the **Hotel Blankenburg**, located on the north edge of town. The hotel is efficiently operated by two generations of the Henzel family. Its 38 comfortable rooms are decorated in a modern style, with dark wood cabinets, furniture and trim. Though not large, the rooms offer many amenities: radio, TV, mini-bar and telephone.

The most appealing room in the hotel is its restaurant, the **Kräutergarten**. *Kräutergarten* means herb garden and, true to its name, the restaurant adjoins a garden where many of the herbs, spices and vegetables used in the kitchen are grown. This oasis of German *Kreative Küche* is one of the most inviting and warmly-decorated dining rooms we've seen. Beamed ceilings, banquettes and furniture are in light pine. The floor is laid with huge, dark tiles. White walls are scattered with a variety of paintings, cooking utensils and lamps. There are jars of herb vinegar and arrangements of dried herbs and spices. An open fireplace with raised hearth, flanked on both sides by neatly stacked firewood adds the final touch of rusticity to this immensely charming room.

Waldhotel Polisina

#22

Marktbreiter Straße 265
D-8701 Frickenhausen
West Germany
Telephone: 09331/3081
Singles 115DM to 145DM
Doubles 150DM to 190DM
Major cards.

The **Waldhotel Polisina** is a good base from which to explore the vineyards of Franconia and to dine — and drink the local vintners' products — at a pair of moderately-priced, but excellent, restaurants in the nearby medieval village of Iphofen.

Set in the trees above the river Main, some 20 kilometers outside Würzburg, the Waldhotel Polisina impresses the first-time visitor with its Teutonic solidity. The entry and hall are a series of rock arches over polished stone floors softened by expanses of Oriental rugs. The beamed ceilings and furniture are of dark wood. The dining room is warmed by a fireplace and rich wood paneling.

Guest rooms continue this feeling with dark brown woodwork and carpets, drapes and bed covers in soft earth tones. Bathrooms are fully tiled and a few of the larger rooms have huge, round, spa-like tubs. On warm days, meals and snacks can be taken outdoors on a pleasant terrace under the trees.

With just 33 rooms, the Polisina is a relatively small hotel. Nonetheless, it offers an array of facilities, from indoor swimming pool, solarium and sauna to tennis courts. The hotel is quietly situated with walking destinations in all directions.

Perhaps the best feature of the Polisina is its proximity to the town of Iphofen, some 15 or 16 kilometers through the old town of Marktbreit, and its two fine country restaurants, the **Romantik Hotel Zehntkeller** and the **Zur Iphofer Kammer**.

This area is also one of the main wine-growing regions in Germany. The misconception about German wines is that they are always white and sweet. Not so. Franken wines are sometimes red and dry to the point of steeliness. Though little known in this country, one often finds them on restaurant wine lists in Germany. You will see them in their squat, dark green bottles: *bocksbeutel*. Try them.

Hotel Abtei

#23

Abteistraße 14
D-2000 Hamburg 13
West Germany
Telephone: 040/442905
Fax: 040/449820
Singles 130DM to 170DM
Doubles 180DM to 314DM
Breakfast 18DM per person
Major Cards.

The best little hotels of Europe are invariably the creation of a single mind; one able to visualize the finished product in detail, and possessed of enough good taste, management skill, energy and stamina to make it happen. Sometimes the visionary lived 200 years ago and the family continues a tradition. Occasionally, a third, fourth or 10th generation in a hotel family can transform the ordinary into something special.

For those of us who revel in small hotel discoveries, the best of all worlds is when the person whose idea the hotel was in the first place — who chose every picture, every knife, every fork, every bottle of wine in the cellar — is there at the door when we arrive.

Such a person is Fritz Lay, collector of small antique tables and maker of exquisite porcelain wash bowls, whose 14-room **Hotel Abtei** has become the Hamburg hideaway for such rich and famous as former tennis great Bjorn Borg and NBC newsman, John Chancellor. The Abtei is on a quiet street of fine old homes in the Harvesthude section of Hamburg near the northwest shore of the Outer Alster, perhaps a 30 minute walk from the Rathaus.

The awninged white building that houses the Abtei looks like many of the other noble old homes on the street, and was built in 1893. Herr Lay turned it into a hotel 12 years ago. Chosen with care and taste from auctions and antique dealers all over Europe, particularly in England, are pieces of furniture and fine pictures, including at least one George Romney painting. One remarkable item in the little parlor is a four-panel screen containing a delightful collage of pictures which were sold door-to-door by British school children during World War I to support the war effort.

The rear of the house looks onto a restful little garden where breakfast, tea and in-between snacks are taken when the weather is good. Speaking of breakfast, though not included in the price of the room, it is bountiful and delicious. Pastry is baked daily on the premises, including what Herr Lay says is the best *brioche* in Hamburg. Coffee is individually brewed to order, and the orange juice is fresh.

Guest rooms are distinctive and come in varying sizes, shapes and decor. Antiques abound. Room Number 2 has a pair of big windows which overlook the garden and a quirky oil-on-tin painting in which the clock in the picture actually keeps time. Each room has an excellent stereo system and Herr Lay provides a dozen classical music tapes which he personally selected and recorded. Some of the bathrooms, as in suite Number 10, have the wonderful hand-painted porcelain fixtures which are made by the company in which Herr Lay is a partner.

Don't go through your travel agent to book the Abtei, because Herr Lay deals with only a handful he knows personally. One has the feeling he would like to select his guests the way he chooses pieces of antique furniture — to fit the hotel. That is not to say he is stuffy or haughty. On the contrary, he is a down-to-earth sort who will rattle on all day to anyone who shows the slightest interest in any of his passions: the Abtei, porcelain, antique furniture, music and, no doubt, several more. It's just that he insists everything go right at his hotel.

AIRPORT HOTELS

The choice of where to stay on the last night of a European trip is an important one. Whether the departure day journey to the airport is by rental car, train, taxi or hotel shuttle, it needs to be relatively short. You want to feel confident about boarding the flight home rested, relaxed and with time to spare, perhaps for some last minute shopping at the airport.

We like to stay away from airport hotels, they usually lack charm and are expensive. Sometimes, however, one is forced to spend the last night at one of these establishments, simply because it seems there is no better nearby alternative. Here are two fine country hotels only minutes from the Frankfurt Airport.

Hotel Birkenhof #24

von Eiff Straße 37
D-6450 Hanau 7 (Steinheim)
West Germany
Telephone: 06181/6461
Singles 80DM to 95DM
Doubles 130DM to 150DM
American Express, Diner's Club.

The **Hotel Birkenhof** is in the Steinheim district of Hanau, about 20 minutes east and a bit north of the airport.

Three things particularly recommend the Birkenhof. The first is the welcome extended by its bustling owner/manager, Frau Fichtner. She is friendly, capable, hospitable — and fluent in several languages, including English and Russian.

Another pleasant feature of this little hotel is its handsome, high-ceilinged dayroom with tall, wide windows overlooking the garden. This room's large fireplace is the perfect spot for a final hot chocolate or brandy before turning in.

The plentiful food, cooked and served under the supervision of the meticulous Frau Fichtner, is the third reason to stay at the Birkenhof. (Dinner is for guests only.)

Located in a residential neighborhood, the hotel is a few minutes walk from a walled enclave of buildings which includes a medieval castle. All the buildings within the walls are presently undergoing restoration by the German government.

The Birkenhof is small (15 rooms) and not easy to find. But, once located, there is no problem getting to the airport the next day. After leaving the hotel, turn left on Darmstädter Straße to B45, then left to the A3 autobahn. By this time you will see signs for the *Flughafen*.

Hotel Sonnenhof

#25

Falkensteiner Straße 9
D-6240 Königstein im Taunus
West Germany
Telephone: 06174/29080
Telex: 410636
Singles 100DM to 135DM
Doubles 142DM to 220DM
Major cards except Visa.

Though a bit more removed from the airport (35 minutes opposed to 20 for the Birkenhof), and substantially more expensive, the **Hotel Sonnenhof** in Königstein im Taunus is a wonderful place to spend your last night in Europe. Though not so posh as its more celebrated neighbor, the **Schloß-Hotel Kronberg**, the Sonnenhof is definitely a luxury choice. We don't think of it as an airport hotel, but more as a fine country hotel that also happens to be conveniently located.

Like a country estate, the Sonnenhof is beautifully placed on extensive, well-tended grounds in the midst of the Taunus mountains. You will enjoy walking down the wide lawns and among the trees, pausing from time to time to look back at the handsome turreted hotel.

The large, high-ceilinged rooms all have views of the surrounding hills or the Main river valley.

The Sonnenhof's restaurant, with outdoor dining under large umbrellas, is elegant, pricey and offers an extensive wine list. Dinner for two persons, without wine, will range from about 100 to 160DM.

Romantik Hotel Bierhütte

Romantik Hotel Bierhütte

#26

D-8351 Hohenau
West Germany
Telephone: 08558/315
Singles 72DM to 95DM
Doubles 104DM to 195DM
Major cards except Visa.

    The Bavarian Forest is an area not much frequented by Americans, though it's difficult to understand why: it is a lovely, quiet region with several very good — but not too expensive — hotels. One of the best is the **Romantik Hotel Bierhütte**, only a few kilometers from Germany's only national forest, the *Nationalpark Bayerischerwald*, with its extensive network of footpaths and hiking trails.

    At the Bierhütte you know you are in the country because the hotel shares its plaza with two busy farms. On a recent visit the warm air was rich with the smells of haying, a task that went on from early morning until dusk.

    Rooms are spacious, trimmed with knotty pine and comfortably furnished with sofa, easy chair and writing desk. Ground floor bedrooms of the guest house have sliding glass doors opening onto a protected terrace with chaise lounges and a wide lawn which slopes gently to a small lake. In the guest-house's hospital-clean basement are sauna, solarium and gym. The main building occupies the site of an ancient brewery that dates to 1535. Its sparkling public rooms are unmistakably Bavarian, with white vaulted ceilings decorated in the Rococo style.

    The Bierhütte is an excellent example of what makes travel in the German countryside so enjoyable; it is a perfect place to relax in serene surroundings, passing the days with long walks, naps and paperback novels. The city of Passau, picturesquely positioned on a narrow peninsula at the confluence of the rivers Danube, Inn and Ilz, is about half an hour's drive away. Cozy evenings are spent in the rustic dining room, enjoying first-rate German food (with *nouvelle* leanings), good beer and wine. When the air is warm and still, heavy with the aroma of animals and haying from the nearby farms, and one is reclining on a chaise, a cool beer at hand, the words *"Summertime, and the livin' is easy..."* may come to mind.

Hotel Hirschgasse

#27

Hirschgasse 3
D-6900 Heidelberg
West Germany
Telephone: 06221/4032160
Fax: 06221/4032196
Singles 265DM to 450DM
Doubles 295DM to 450DM
Breakfast 21 DM per person
Major Cards.

Heidelberg is one of Germany's must-see towns. The view from across the Neckar river to the old town and the Schloß above it is one we never tire of. Its best small hotel is the **Hirschgasse**.

In the late 70s and early 80s we found it a good first stop after a long flight, Heidelberg being only about an hour's drive from the Frankfurt airport. We used to arrive mid-day, nap until evening, then walk across the Neckar over the *Alte Brucke* for dinner. However, a fire closed the hotel from January of 1988 until May of 1989 and the Kraft family took that opportunity to transform a quaint inn with 45 smallish guest rooms into a stunning little treasure of a hotel of just 15 suites and three studio apartments. It is no longer an appetizer but a main course of a hotel.

The Hirschgasse is an historic guest house dating from 1472 and that atmosphere has always been its most appealing feature. Little of that feeling was lost in the fire (mainly smoke damage) and a great deal gained in the renovation.

Located on a hillside in a neighborhood of handsome old homes, the Hirschgasse looks the same from the outside as before the fire: a three story building with dormer windows in the roof, yellow stucco, green shutters and bountiful boxes of red geraniums at each window. Inside the changes are not especially noticeable until one sees the guest rooms.

The London design firm of Laura Ashley was hired to decorate and the result is 18 dazzling chambers, each with a unique decorative theme mainly achieved through the use of color and a variety of fabrics. For example, the *Paisley Suite*, decorated in the style of an English country house, has furniture covered in dark leather, thick dark red carpeting and a bathroom tiled in white with blue trim. Bathrobes provided in this suite are pink and blue. Hand-crocheted coverlets are spread over the two large beds. The drapes are paisley, and paisley table covers hang to the floor. This a two bedroom suite and could accommodate four adults.

The *Peking Suite* shows off some of the family's antique Asian furniture, including a great canopied bed. The room also has three stained-glass windows which look onto the garden. The *Schloß Suite* offers a view of the Castle across the Neckar. Some suites such as the *Malven* (hollyhocks) are on two levels, with the parlor and bedroom connected by a staircase.

The big bathrooms are superb. All have a separate room for the toilet and in each there is both a shower and a large tub with Jacuzzi. Towels hang on antique wooden racks built in London near the turn of the century, to dry clothing in front of a fireplace.

Despite the changes, the hotel's bloodlines are preserved. Where there were dormer windows before there are still dormer windows. Many antiques remain from the old house and it seems no two rooms have the same physical layout or view. Other touches, such as exposing a section of the original half-timbered wall, also remind us that someone was handing out room keys here 20 years before Columbus set sail.

The restaurant, **Le Gourmet**, has also been upgraded and now offers a higher cuisine served in an immensely warm and inviting setting. Rough wood beams intersect the ancient polished planks of the 500 year-old original ceiling. The pre-fire leaded glass windows are still there, as are the stone walls. But instead of bare wood tables, as before the fire, there is white linen and candlelight.

We expect the Hirschgasse to soon occupy a spot among the very top small hotels in Germany.

Germany

MEERSBURG

If Walt Disney had designed a German village, he might have produced something like Meersburg: cobbled streets, flower-filled plazas, half-timbered houses, a tower gate, giant mill wheel, a tiny harbor at the lakeshore and a medieval castle overlooking it all. But Meersburg isn't Disneyland. Real people live in those half-timbered houses, a family occupies the castle, children go to school at the *Gymnasium*.

The romantic nature of Meersburg draws many visitors. In late spring and summer, especially on weekends, the village is packed with Germans on holiday. They come to play in the lake, drink the local wine and relax in the handful of hotels and vacation houses in and around town.

Compared with Lindau, its more famous neighbor down the lake, Meersburg is a little downscale. The hotels are generally simpler, less luxurious and less expensive. Most restaurants serve traditional German food; Lindau has several establishments which fall in the *Kreative Küche* category. Though prices are lower here, Meersburg is no less lovely and is well worth a visit

Villa Bellevue #28

Am Rosenhag 5
D-7758 Meersburg
West Germany
Telephone: 07532/9770
Singles 78DM to 90DM
Doubles 145DM to 190DM
Major cards except Visa.

The **Villa Bellevue** is a short walk from the center of town and as such is absolutely quiet. Owner Fritz Brandner is usually on hand to make certain his guests are happy and comfortable; not a difficult job given the *gemütlich* atmosphere he has created.

The hotel is on a plateau overlooking the lake; upper floor rooms have terraces, lower floor rooms lead directly to a sloping lawn/garden. Beds are some of the most comfortable we have encountered. Add to their comfort the silence of being away from the bustle of Meersburg's center, and you are practically guaranteed a good night's sleep.

Rooms are average-sized, but well laid-out with comfortable sitting areas. Each has a small outdoor table in order to take breakfast in the morning sun. Because it is only an easy five to ten minute walk to the center of the village, and its guest rooms are the best in town, the Villa Bellevue is our first choice in Meersburg.

Germany

THE ISLAND OF SYLT

Sylt is a skinny strip of heather-covered dunes sitting in the North Sea off the coasts of Germany and Denmark. The Germans — and practically nobody else — flock here by the thousands in the summer, taking the cure at the giant oceanside *Kurhaus,* eating at the many fine restaurants on the island and exploring the dunes and beaches.

Locals tout fall visits; a time, they say, when the weather is best. Winter, when prices are lower and magnificent storms roll in from the Arctic to pound the rocky beaches, would also be a good time to escape here for a few days. Dress for the cold and take bracing walks on the promenade along the ocean, then come inside to warm yourself by a fire with a hot drink and a good book and the anticipation of a hearty meal.

Benen-Diken Hof

#29

Süderstraße
D-2280 Keitum/Sylt
West Germany
Telephone: 04651/31035
Telex: 221252
Singles 170DM to 290DM
Doubles 190DM to 360DM
Major cards.

Our choice, in any season, would be the **Benen-Diken Hof**, one of the best small hotels anywhere in the world.

In 1973, Claas Johannsen, a Frisian farmer, opened his *insel auf der insel* (island on the island). He is still there, watching and overseeing all, pouring drinks for a dozen or so guests each evening in the hotel's cozy, elegant bar. It is a duty he shares only with his efficient and dedicated manager, Cornelia Starck. He could easily hire a bartender but is firm about maintaining personal contact with guests. Rooms don't have mini-bars because Herr Johannsen thinks it keeps guests in

Benen–Diken Hof

The 50 Best Country Inns & Small, City Hotels

their rooms. There is, however, an honor-system refrigerator where, at any hour, guests may choose from a full range of beverages.

Nothing is dark, old or traditional about the Benen-Diken Hof. Oh, there are some lovely antiques, including an 800-year old grandfather clock, and the welcome and service are in the best tradition of German hostelry, but the principal feeling is one of light, space and air. For example, the walk to rooms in the new part of the hotel (an addition was built in 1983) is down a corridor where one wall is entirely floor-to-ceiling sliding glass panels. These open to an inner courtyard. The large, modern rooms are decorated in light, neutral shades with light, wood-trimmed furniture. French doors are everywhere, opening to terraces, lawns and balconies.

All the rooms are superb, but the two we like best are Number 33 (the "most loved room in the house and seldom free") and the small suite, Number 47.

A small but exquisite card room — whose beautifully-paneled walls display 100-year old paintings of sailing ships — would be perfect for an after-dinner rubber of bridge. For children there is a well-equipped playroom. The whirlpool, sauna and indoor swimming pool all sparkle.

Outside, the hotel's gleaming white thatched-roof buildings are gathered at the end of a white-fenced gravel lane. One or two sheep graze the wide front lawns. Except for the thatched roofs, it brings to mind a prosperous Kentucky thoroughbred farm.

The Benen-Diken Hof is not undiscovered in Germany. In fact, in 1987 it was named the country's finest hotel *garni* (without restaurant). This designation is a bit misleading because there is, in fact, a delightful restaurant. Mornings it serves a giant buffet breakfast that includes, in part: six kinds of sausage, three kinds of ham, five different breads, five varieties of jams and jellies and a half dozen juices. Yogurts, jams and jellies are all made on the premises. In the evenings there is a small menu, for house guests only, consisting of lighter fare such as soups, seafood cocktails and cold dishes. On fine days, one can take breakfast or a snack outside in the courtyard under its giant umbrella.

Everything in the hotel bears the stamp of Herr Johannsen, from the paintings on the walls to the way your beer is poured. With taste, personal charm and attention to detail, he has created one of the great hotels of the world.

Advance booking is essential. Rooms in summer are often reserved a year in advance, and even in winter you should not expect to drop in without calling ahead. And bring warm clothing no matter what time of year you go; weather can be blustery even in high summer and quite severe in the dead of winter.

Restaurant Tip:

The **Käpt'n Hahn** is in the island's largest village (population 9000), Westerland. The food is splendid and the portions generous — haute cuisine for the German appetite. Capable staff, never rushed, in an easy atmosphere, not stuffy or affected. If the Käpt'n Hahn doesn't qualify as a great restaurant, we're not sure of the requirements.

Hotel Anker

#30

Obertorstraße 6
Postfach 106
D-8772 Marktheidenfeld
West Germany
Telephone: 093391/4041
Telex: 689608
Singles 90DM to 100DM
Doubles 130 to 240DM
Major Cards.

The town of Marktheidenfeld, in the Franconian wine country a few miles north of Würzburg, isn't in the guidebooks and its **Hotel Anker** is hardly chic or even charming in that cute, Sound of Music way which characterizes so many small hotels in Germany, Austria and Switzerland. To be sure, it offers plenty of solid, Germanic comfort, but what raises the Anker above dozens of similar hotels whose physical attributes equal or outstrip it, is its management.

The Deppisches have been in the hotel and wine business in Marktheidenfeld since 1872. All family members we have had the good fortune to meet exude a special air of friendly professionalism that is the common denominator of the best small European hotels. When you check in and are shown to your room, it's almost as though they've been waiting for you to arrive. Immediately, you feel welcome and at home — yet without any loss of privacy.

Don't get the wrong impression from the first sentence of this review, the Anker is a Mercedes Benz of a hotel: solid, not flashy, but everything works and is built to last. Located just a block or two from a walk along the banks of the Main river, the hotel is arranged around an inner courtyard. At night, the arched gates are closed and one has the feeling of being tucked safely into a protected little enclave. Part of the hotel's perimeter was once a portion of the town wall.

Rooms are large with dark wood furniture made by hand especially for the hotel. Bathrooms are spacious and everything is spotless. Attention has been paid to detail at the Anker; reading lamps are excellent and your automobile occupies its own one-car garage.

Service is faultless. The first morning of your stay, Karoline Deppisch is likely to escort you to your table in the breakfast room. Want a beer and a sandwich at the picnic table under the big tree in the inner courtyard? What a favor you're doing them to request it! And everybody — that's *everybody* — smiles at every contact.

And, when you walk across the street for lunch or dinner at the Deppisch family's **Weinhaus Anker**, it only gets better. The several dining rooms strike a wonderful compromise between elegance and *gemütlichkeit*. The service equals that found at the hotel, and the food justfiably gets a Michelin star. A small bouquet of fresh flowers accompanies the arrival of each course. Wine is drunk from delicate, long-stemmed glasses, the china is Rosenthal.

The Anker is just an hour from the Frankfurt airport and makes an excellent first or last stop on your trip, or is an ideal base from which to explore Würzburg and the Franconian countryside.

Berghotel Latscheneck

#31

Kaffeefeld 1
D-8102 Mittenwald
West Germany
Telephone: 08823/1419
Singles 105DM to 115DM
Doubles 210DM to 230DM
Prices half-board
No cards.

There are some hotels one simply doesn't want to leave. Perhaps it's the comfortable rooms, the good food or the wonderful service. Though all these virtues apply to the **Berghotel Latscheneck**, the main reason for our wanting to stay was the fear of driving back down the narrow, steep road we had negotiated in terror two nights before, trying to avoid the icy patches. (In the daylight, the trip was much less daunting.)

The Latscheneck sits on a small, flat bit of land above Mittenwald, commanding spectacular views of both the Wetterstein and Karwendel ranges. Many of its guests come faithfully, some for two weeks each summer, then again for two more in the winter; hiking in the warm weather along the many trails which criss-cross the region, skiing during the colder months.

As a town, charming little Mittenwald can be done in half a day: walk the streets around the parish church and look at the fine examples of Bavarian painted houses — some of the most beautiful and detailed painted buildings in Germany are in Mittenwald. Walk through the small *Geigenbaumuseum* (violin museum) and inspect the small, rococo parish church. Notice especially the carving on the pews and the mural paintings by Matthäus Günther.

Most of the guests at the Latscheneck seem to ignore the "urban" pleasures of Mittenwald, concentrating instead on the outdoor activities around the hotel. Every morning guests come to breakfast dressed in hiking gear, ready for the walking paths leading from the hotel. Some, though, prefer to stay around the house, reading and relaxing.

The hotel is basic Alpen style, with a low-pitched roof and balconies off many rooms. To find the Latscheneck, follow the signs to the main chairlift above town; near the chair you will see signs to the hotel. As you drive into the parking area, expect Klaus Neuner to open a window, stick out his head and shout *Grüss Gott* before running down to help with your bags. Expect this kind of personal attention to continue: the Latscheneck has only 16 rooms and the Neuners (Klaus and his mother run the place) work hard to make sure your every need is met. Klaus is the more outgoing of the two and speaks better English.

Much of the common area is decorated with color photographs taken by Herr Neuner, who, during the months the Latscheneck is closed, travels the world taking photographs which he assembles into high-tech slide shows for theaters. Judging from the clippings on the wall, Klaus Neuner has achieved some level of fame in Germany for his art.

Rooms are comfortable and beautifully maintained. All are typically Bavarian: white plaster walls, light wood ceiling, open beams, etc. The beds feature fluffy down comforters and thick pillows, perfect for collapsing into after a day of hiking — or even a day of napping. Most rooms have a small table for those wishing to take breakfast in the room, play a hand of cards or write letters.

If you make reservations far enough in advance, ask for one of the larger rooms, such as Number Eight, Number Six or Number Three, as the price per person is only about 10% to 15% higher than the smaller accommodations.

Dinner is included with the price of rooms and we were pleasantly surprised at the quality of the meals.

Gemütlichkeit is a difficult term to translate, but the Berghotel Latscheneck definitely has it.

The hotel is closed during April until late May and from mid-October to just before Christmas each year.

Hotel Feiler

#32

Oberer Markt 4
D-8551 Muggendorf
West Germany
Telephone: 091/963 22
Singles 85DM to 110DM
Doubles 130DM to 180DM
American Express, Diners Club.

There are two things one should probably not attempt to describe about the **Hotel Feiler**: its interior and the taste of its wild mushrooms.

Located on a quiet street in Muggendorf, a small town in the region known as Swiss Franconia, an hour north of Nürnberg, the hotel is an intriguing stone and half-timbered country cottage. The roof is red tile and the window boxes burst with colorful flowers. With just 12 guest rooms and a somewhat eccentric — but appealing — interior, the Feiler is comfortable, quiet and curious.

Inside is a hodge-podge of fine furniture, antiques, Victorian red-plush accents, tanks of colorful fish and a zoo of stuffed animals and birds. One of its most appealing nooks is a small, but particularly charming inner courtyard (see cover) overlooked by flower-bedecked balconies and windows — a fine place to lunch in good weather. A caution to some is the presence of dozens of stuffed critters which populate the Feiler's public rooms, including the restaurant. Far more appealing is the sweet chime of a grandfather clock, heard each half-hour.

Guest rooms are romantic. Number 15 is snug and *gemütlich* with a four-poster, canopied bed, bunches of dried flowers in copper vessels, heavy beamed ceiling (no nails, just wooden pegs hold it together), built-in bookshelves and five windows cut into the thick walls.

The best feature of the Feiler, however, is its restaurant. Horst Feiler takes justifiable pride in his mushrooms, which are picked in the nearby forests by a handful of trusted and expert gatherers, including Herr Feiler himself. The dishes which these fungi become are exquisite, subtle, beautifully-presented and generally indescribable. Also rela-

Hotel Feiler

The 50 Best Country Inns & Small, City Hotels

tively expensive; expect to pay 140-190DM for two at dinner, not including wine.

A SHORT DRIVE TO THE HOTEL FEILER

This drive to the **Hotel Feiler** in Muggendorf is from Autobahnroute #5, heading north from Nürnberg toward Bayreuth. *Deutsche Generalkarte* #17 is the map for this area and will be helpful, especially should you wish to explore some of the other roads and villages of Swiss Franconia.

Leave the autobahn at the Pegnitz/Grafenwöhr exit and proceed west toward Pottenstein and Forcheim. Approximately 1.4 kilometers later make the left turn, again toward Pottenstein. Then at 3.7 kilometers is the right turn onto Red Road #470.

At this point the drive is through rolling countryside alternating stands of forest with pastures and farms. At 6.0 kilometers is the village of Wannberg and, at 8.9 kilometers into the drive, the road descends to a steep-sided canyon. On the left are the attractive ponds of a fish farm.

From here to your destination in Muggendorf, the drive winds through the rocky, enclosed canyon. Most of the vegetation is deciduous, making this journey especially lovely in the fall.

Shortly you will see the *Teufelshöhe*, a series of caves whose entrance is forty or fifty feet above the roadway on your left. The guided tour takes about 45 minutes, costs a few marks and requires warm clothing.

A calm lake, suitable for relaxed boating and fishing, is 10 kilometers into the drive.

At the town of Pottenstein you will be interested in the old buildings perched on the edge of outcroppings of rock, balanced precariously upon each other, overhanging the town at a height of 100-200 feet.

As the road winds through the canyon it crosses and re-crosses the pretty Püttlachtal, a river which keeps changing its look. One moment it is fast and bubbling, the next, fat, slow and smooth.

Tüchersfeld has a most extraordinary setting: Numerous vertical rock pillars rise — seeming almost to grow — several stories vertically out of the town. Its stores and homes are scattered among them. You may wish to stop for a few minutes for picture taking.

Muggendorf is 26.5 kilometers from the autobahn. To reach the hotel, drive all the way through the town and make the right turn rather than the sharp left toward Forcheim.

MUNICH

Those who saw the pile of rubble which Allied bombers made of Munich in 1945 must now marvel at what the city has become. Elegant and affluent, it seems to bear no outward trace of wartime destruction. Munich possesses a unique freshness, its air is clean, its streets are spotless. It is a city of sleek motorcars and handsome people.

Nearly every first-time visitor to Germany heads to Munich. So do travelers on their second trip. And those on their third, fourth and fifth. The city attracts for many reasons: its proximity to the Alps and Germany's royal castles, its museums, its food and its beer. Munich is modern, yet at nearly every corner one is reminded this is a city which dates from the ninth century. But most of all, Munich has what all great cities have: a special aura of excitement and anticipation.

Perhaps more than any other city in Germany, Munich offers the kind of well-located, charming little hotels one finds in cities such as Paris and Vienna.

Hotel Prinzregent

The 50 Best Country Inns & Small, City Hotels

Hotel Prinzregent

#33

Ismaninger Straße 42-44,
D-8000 München 80
West Germany
Telephone: 089/4702081
Telex: 524403 prinz d
Fax: 89/4702392
Singles 190DM to 250DM
Doubles 250DM to 280DM
Studios 305DM to 360DM
Major cards.

The lobby and common areas of the **Hotel Prinzregent** are the most outstanding example of traditional Bavarian architecture we've seen even though the hotel is just five years old and the interiors are from Switzerland, not Bavaria. When the hotel was built, the owners found an old Swiss inn which was being demolished. Its hundred-year-old interiors were dismantled and trucked to Munich where Herr Eyrer, the city's most respected interior decorator specializing in the Bavarian style, supervised their re-installation.

The result is spectacular. The large breakfast room with wide plank floors, carved wooden banquettes, and sturdy but elegant tables, is a warm, comfortable place to take your morning repast. A few carved wooden figures are placed throughout the room. The buffet is bountiful, and on warm days the wide doors are opened onto a garden terrace; you can either stay inside to enjoy the infusion of fresh air, or eat at one of the tables outdoors.

Off the lobby is a small, comfortable bar which feels almost like a wooden cave. Every surface seems to be covered with light wood: floors, walls, ceiling, the bar itself. One of the most interesting features is a row of glass tankards hanging at one end of the bar. Above each mug, carved in the wood, is the name of the regular to whom it belongs: Anton, Joseph, Hans, Peter and several others. Even if you don't stay in the Prinzregent, you might want to stop in for a drink and see this lovely little room.

Though guestrooms are on the small side, we rate them adequate in that regard. Furnishings do not differ from room to room; all have carved wood headboards and bed tables, a small sitting area and chest of drawers. A brightly-patterned brocade fabric is used as bedspread, upholstery and curtains. All rooms have color TV with cable and telephone; baths feature magnifying mirrors and heated towel racks.

The service provided by the hotel's attractive staff is excellent.

The Prinzregent is located in the Bogenhausen section of Munich, across the Isar river, not far from the Deutsches Museum.

Hotel Exquisit

#34

Pettenkoferstraße 3
D-8000 München 2
West Germany
Telephone: 089/5519900
Telex: 529863
Fax: 89/55199499
Singles 160DM
Doubles 220DM
Suites 280DM
Major cards.

Make early reservations for the **Hotel Exquisit**, because with just 48 rooms and reasonable rates, it's bound to be booked far in advance. Everything seems to be right about the Exquisit: service, decor, location, amenities, etc.

The hotel is owned by veteran restaurateur Manfred Vollmer, owner of one of our favorite Munich beer restaurants, the **Augustiner Gastätten**. Vollmer has created a hotel which, with time, could become the best in the city, combining elegant but comfortable rooms, excellent but understated service, and fine cuisine. The Exquisit is on a quiet side street near the Sendlinger Tor, within walking distance of the *Hauptbahnhof* and the Marienplatz.

Light, airy colors accented by fine, dark wood predominate in the guest rooms. Baths have nearly every amenity and were designed so two people can comfortably prepare for an evening out, with plenty of space and double sinks. Thirsty terry robes are set out for you. Beds are firm and inviting with fluffy, high quality down comforters and pillows.

Number 202 is a fine double with a small terrace, but our favorite room in the house is Number 456. This is a corner "maisonette" on two levels: downstairs is a living room with a comfortable sofa and chairs and color television. Up a set of curving stairs is a loft bedroom. An excellent value for 280DM a night.

Service equals that of any hotel in town. When you pull up in your car to check in, a porter will take it to the underground garage

(12DM per day extra) and, if you wish, have it washed, waxed or filled with gas. An extra charge applies to these services, of course. Transportation to and from the train station or airport is also available, as are chauffeured limousines. The front desk staff is thoroughly professional and ready to see to your every need.

Unfortunately, we did not dine at the Exquisit, but based on head chef Bernard Thierry's reputation and resumé, we would expect the quality of the cuisine to match that of the hotel. Before coming to oversee the kitchen at the Exquisit, Thierry worked at such culinary palaces at Auberge de l'Ill, Aubergine, Tantris and La Tour d'Argent.

Breakfast is from the buffet, and Chef Thierry oversees this meal as well, so expect something special. There is a bakery and full-time baker on staff, so rolls and other breads are fresh every morning.

The Exquisit could become your favorite hotel in Munich.

Hotel An der Oper

#35

Falkenturmstraße 10
D-8000 München 2
Telephone: 089/228711
Telex: 522588
Singles 105DM to 140DM
Doubles 165DM to 182DM
Major cards.

    The **Hotel An der Oper** is on quiet Falkenturmstraße, just off Maximilianstraße, the city's luxury shopping district. It is just steps from the opera house and the **Hofbräuhaus** and only a few blocks from the Marienplatz.

    The 55-room An der Oper is modern in style and decoration, but a few classical touches here and there stave off the feeling of sterility that pervades many "contemporary" hotels. Rooms are relatively small, but comfortable and soundproof. The staff is helpful and friendly.

    Though not in the category of some of the other small city hotels in this book, the An der Oper is nevertheless our first choice among the Munich's moderately priced establishments. Make reservations far in advance; the An der Oper is heavily booked.

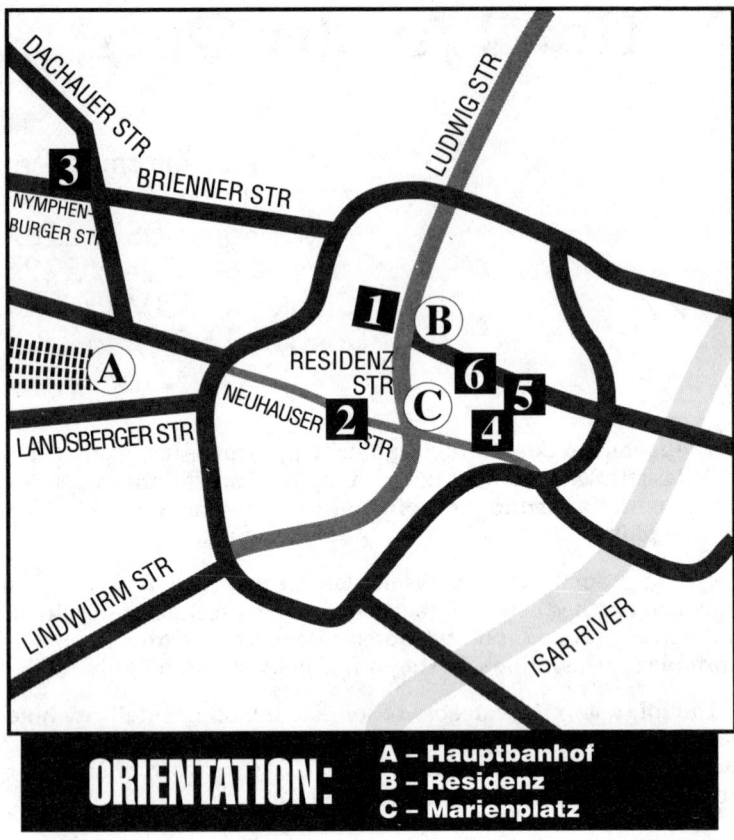

BEER RESTAURANTS OF MUNICH

Munich's beer restaurants, owned and operated by the city's several major breweries, offer excellent food at good prices. Here, briefly, are some of our thoughts regarding these Munich institutions.

Augustiner Gaststätten, 16 Neuhauser Straße: **2** It is, of course, a matter of personal taste, but we put this beer house at the top of the heap. We once drove from the Frankfurt Airport in less than three hours in order to arrive before the restaurant closed to get the mixed grill. It is said beer was first brewed on this spot in the 14th century. The beer is still served but, sad to report, the mixed grill is no longer on the menu. In our view, though, this is the best of the beer restaurants.

Spatenhaus, Residenzstraße 12: **1** Overlooking the Opera House on Max-Joseph Platz and attracting an after-opera clientele, Spatenhaus is a cut above Munich's other beer restaurants in style and price. In substance, however, it is not. Tables are difficult to come by and we have found the service, food and the welcome (particularly in the tonier upstairs restaurant) uneven. To be fair, on some occasions the food has been excellent and the service prompt and friendly; it just isn't that way consistently. However, we rate the beer right behind Augustiner.

Löwenbräu: At two locations: **5** **3** Löwenbräukeller near the Hofbräuhaus, and Löwenbräu-Stuben, outside the Ring at 2 Nymphenburgerstraße. Known throughout the world, this famous brewery seems to have fallen on hard times. That this proud old brewery would allow the Miller Brewing Company to market, under the Löwenbräu label in this country, a product brewed in Milwaukee, seems indicative of trouble. The food and beer at the restaurant on Stiglmaierplatz are not up to standard and the musical entertainment can be downright embarrassing. Recent visits have found a lot of customers disguised as empty tables.

Hofbräuhaus, Platzl 9: **4** The huge, smoky ground floor hall of this Munich institution must be seen at least once, even if all you do is wander in for a quick look around. This is world-class people watching. American college students who have had far too much beer, Japanese tourists and worse-for-wear local habitues are served liters of beer by iron-armed women with a tired look that says, "Nothing you can do or say surprises me, I've seen it all." All are watched over by a cadre of bouncers and entertained by a lively band which plays far too intermittently. The food and entertainment on the two floors above are more refined.

Haxnbauer, Münzstraße 2: **6** It has been our experience that the many tourists attracted to the Haxnbauer are rather brusquely dealt with. Nonetheless, this place is worth enduring the rudeness at least once for the delicious speciality of the house, spit-roasted *schweinshaxn* or *kalbshaxn* (pork or veal hock/shank).

Gutshotel des Weingutes

Gutshotel des Weingutes

#36

Balduinstraße 1
D-559 Neumagen-Dhron
West Germany
Telephone: 06507/2035
Singles 98DM
Doubles 136DM to 150DM
Mastercard.

The natural inclination when touring the Mosel is to start at either Koblenz or Trier and go from one to the other with an overnight stop, or possibly two, somewhere in the middle. The **Gutshotel des Weingutes Reichgraf von Kesselstatt** in Neumagen-Dhron will make you re-evaluate that strategy.

Once you've seen this lovely little inn, which has several advantages of a major hotel — fine restaurant, indoor pool, sauna and tennis court — you may be tempted to explore the river in both directions with the Gutshotel des Weingutes as your headquarters. And, since there is a road on both sides of the river, you won't have to do much retracing of steps. Trier is 39 kilometers south, Bernkastel-Kues is 20 kilometers north and Koblenz is about 100 kilometers beyond that.

Until it was purchased by Günther Reh in 1978, the von Kesselstatt family controlled the greatest private family estate of the Mosel-Saar-Ruwer, with about 60 hectares. The von Kesselstatt name is still on the wine labels, and the business — which has grown considerably — is still run from the baroque Kesselstatt palace in Trier. In 1986, Annegret Reh converted one of the von Kesselstatt estates into a 20-room hotel. The pleasant result is Gutshotel des Weingutes, which overlooks the river from the right bank just outside the village of Neumagen.

Ten minutes' walk from the hotel is the little pier where day-trip boats stop for passengers. Easy and pleasant river rides to Trier and Bernkastel-Kues are available — with time for lunch and sightseeing.

This is another of those country inns whose public rooms have the atmosphere and feel of a beautiful private residence rather than a hotel. We stayed in the converted attic, a huge, airy guest room that comprises the entire top floor of the hotel. You open the door to the room before walking up the stairs to the living area. It's like a little flat, with a kitchen, dormer windows on three sides and twin beds at one end. It is perhaps as large as 18 by 40 feet. In the middle is a couch, overstuffed chair, coffee table and television. At the other end is the bathroom and tiny kitchenette. The slanting attic walls are white, the woodwork blond and the floors hardwood. For two persons the price is 150DM. At any price, it is one of the most appealing rooms we've ever had in *any* country hotel. The other guest rooms are also delightful but ask for this one.

The restaurant, which has good food and a long list of von Kesselstatt wines, is in two narrow rooms across the front of the hotel. There are views of the Mosel and access through several French doors to a terrace overlooking the river. Like every other room of the hotel the atmosphere emphasizes light and air rather than Old World dark and heavy.

The beautifully situated Gutshotel des Weingutes offers outstanding value and is a must for Mosel sojourners.

Hotel Petrisberg

#37

Sickingenstraße 11
D-5500 Trier
West Germany
Telephone: 0651/41181.
Singles 70DM to 80DM
Doubles 115DM to 120DM
No cards.

During World War II, the German army established an anti-aircraft battery on a hillside overlooking Trier. Near the site of that gun emplacement was a small hotel operated by the Pantenberg family. In exchange for cases of wine, soldiers helped the family dig a cave shelter in the hillside above the hotel. From the mouth of that cave two young boys, Helmut and Wolfgang Pantenberg, saw the terrifying, for-real fireworks show in which their city was destroyed by Allied bombers.

The Pantenbergs survived those raids and their **Hotel Petrisberg** was not damaged. It is still there today on that hill above the town, secluded among trees and vineyards. Its owners and managers are the brothers, Helmut and Wolfgang, who watched the bombing of Trier from their hillside shelter 43 years ago.

The Petrisberg is strongly recommended. It is exactly the sort of place we had in mind when we began writing this book. It has that special combination of charm, hospitality, quiet setting and value we couldn't wait to tell you about.

The property has been in the family since 1881. The hotel opened in 1933 and the guest house, which has 15 of the hotel's 35 rooms, was built in 1975.

We first stopped at the Petrisberg in 1979. The warmth of the welcome and service have not changed in the 10 year interim. We especially remembered from that first visit the "honor system" cooler of beer and soft drinks near the reception desk. When settling your bill, you simply tell the Pantenbergs what you took. That cooler, available to guests day and night, with no lock or coin operated mechanism required to open it, says volumes about traveling in this part of the world.

The drive through the Petrisberg's gates, up the long tree-lined driveway, will make you think you are entering the grounds of an expensive European hideaway hotel. Wrong. You are entering the grounds of an inexpensive European hideaway.

Stop the car in front of the main entrance and it is likely either Helmut or Wolfgang will appear to help with the luggage. Both speak excellent English and you will be treated as an old friend, quickly registered and shown to one of hotel's spacious and impeccable guest rooms. Those at the front of the hotel have a fine view of the city, those on the back are cooler in summer and look into the trees.

Though the hotel has no restaurant, on our last visit Helmut came up with a couple of delicious mid-afternoon ham sandwiches. Sunday breakfast surpasses many, far more expensive, five-star hotels. It included all the usual German breakfast staples *plus* bacon, an omelette, several juices, wine, mineral water and fresh pound cake. The latter was made by Wolfgang, who bakes all the Petrisberg's bread and rolls.

NÜRNBERG

Compared with Munich, Berlin, Cologne, Heidelberg, et al., Nürnberg is ignored by American vacation travelers. It is attractive in so many respects, one wonders why. The answer may lie in its recent history.

Nürnberg was the seat of Nazism. Though the party was founded in Munich, Nürnberg was the site of its annual mass meetings and it was here in 1935 that the *Reichstag* approved laws which forbade Germans to marry Jews and established the swastika as Germany's flag. Following the war, its path to infamy was ensured when it became the site for the war crimes trials of Hermann Goering, Rudolf Hess and dozens of other Nazi leaders. Unfortunately, the city now seems inextricably linked to this ten-year span of misfortune, rather than to its hundreds of years as one of Germany's most important cultural centers.

The city traces its beginning to 1050. As the years passed it came to be known as the ideal of medieval splendor. Its walls enclosed some of the greatest art and architecture of the period. Albrecht Dürer lived and worked here and the *Meistersingers von Nürnberg* were more than Wagnerian opera characters; they played an important role in the development of music in Germany. The first high school was established here.

Nürnberg was the target of particularly effective Allied bombing raids. The old town was leveled. Its fine half-timbered homes and stone buildings were reduced to a pile of rubble.

Rebuilding began immediately after the war and today the *altstadt* is once again a vibrant city center. Buildings which were restored stand side by side with new structures, obviously modern but designed to blend harmoniously. It is a classic walking town, with something to see around every corner. The people of Nürnberg are as cordial, friendly and helpful as you'll find in Europe.

Nürnberg also has some of Germany's best cuisine, from the *wurst* vendors in the old town to a variety of starred restaurants in the suburbs. For dinner, don't miss the **Gasthof Bammes** in Buch. To us, it represents the very best of German cooking with just the right classic French touches. For lunch you must eat at the **Bratwursthäusle** near St. Sebaldus. In Nürnberg, bratwurst is a venerated food, and the Bratwursthäusle is its temple.

Weinhaus Steichele

#38

Knorrstraße 2
D-8500 Nürnberg 1
Telephone: 0911/204378
Singles 65DM to 80DM
Doubles 100DM to 130DM
American Express.

We think the **Weinhaus Steichele** is the best hotel in the old, walled center of the city. Like many of the buildings in today's Nürnberg, the Steichele was built in the early '50s using modern materials but in a style in keeping with the city's architectural roots. In addition, the hotel has recently added a new wing which, like the hotel itself, is modern but maintains a traditional feeling.

Rooms in the new wing feature handsome light wood furnishings, small but efficiently laid out and well-appointed baths and comfortable beds with high-quality down comforters. Moreover, these rooms are in the quietest part of the hotel.

The breakfast buffet is ample, similar to what you'd find in a country inn. The staff is excellent: friendly, welcoming, efficient — but not intrusive. Dinner in the restaurant is also recommended; be sure to sample some of the many regional wines.

The Steichele also has the best location among hotels in the *altstadt*. The neighborhood is quiet, there is a parking garage nearby and a *U-bahn* stop around the corner. For arrivals by train, the *bahnhof* is nearby, but not within walking distance for those carrying heavy bags.

A NÜRNBERG WALK AND A HEARTY LUNCH

Our favorite cities are walking cities; places where strolling is encouraged, towns where the center is compact enough that it can be easily transitted on foot, large enough so that each new corner turned brings a surprise.

Nürnberg is almost perfect: a day's stroll will take you to the major sights, leaving you plenty of time for a leisurely lunch and to poke around the shops.

Begin your walk at the door of our recommended hotel in Nürnberg, the **Weinhaus Steichele**, on Knorrstraße near the Jakobsplatz. Turn left out the door and go down Knorrstraße until it bears left onto Jakobstraße. Follow this to the corner of Dr. Kurt Schumacher Straße and bear right: in less than a block you will see the **Germanisches Nationalmuseum**. This is our first stop.

Built on and among the ruins of a Carthusian monastery, this museum succeeds in the difficult task of having something for everybody without losing its focus. While there is too much to see here in one day, we suggest you take an hour or two to see some of the highlights: the pocket guide you receive with your admission will give you a basic layout of the museum and help you plan your attack. Our favorites are the medieval and renaissance art collections, with several originals by Albrecht Dürer — something the Albrecht Dürer Museum lacks. We were also fascinated by the collection of musical instruments which includes not only ancient violins, harpsichords and other easily recognizable instruments but also some experimental pieces which are no longer in use. Some of these are very curious-looking. Another favorite is the architectural exhibit on the top floor, which has several full-size reproductions of rooms from German homes and several models illustrating typical German architecture.

Leaving the museum, walk across Dr. Kurt Schumacher Straße and jog left into the Krebsgasse, entering the main pedestrian-only area at Breite Gasse, where you will turn right. At Pfannenschmiedsgasse turn left into the Lorenzerplatz; if it's a sunny day you'll want to step into **St. Lorenz** to enjoy this Gothic church's rose window.

Coming out of the church, head straight down the wide pedestrian-only Karolinenstraße. As you stroll, try to remember that only about 40 years ago, this entire area was rubble: in some ways,

Germany

Nürnberg was the soul of Germany and Allied bombers meant to break that soul with their repeated attacks. The job of reconstruction was done better here than almost anywhere else. Buildings along the Karolinenstraße were built using modern materials and contemporary forms but in historic style, creating a street that is up-to-date yet has one foot firmly planted in the past.

As you cross the Färberstraße into Hefnersplatz, continue on, bearing slightly left until you come to the **Hans-Sachs-Brunnen** (Hans-Sachs Fountain). You can't miss the fountain: about 10 meters in diameter, it is filled with a metal sculpture depicting animals, men and mythical creatures which is almost impossible to describe but quite interesting in a macabre sort of way.

Go back in the direction you came, but angle left into Josephsplatz. Turn right on Adlerstraße, walking past the post office about a block to a double set of stairs called the **Gefallenendenkmal**, which takes you down to Kaiserstraße. Kaiserstraße, which runs both left and right from where you are, and the Unter and Obere Wörthstraßes (which are to your left about a block) is one of the nicer shopping areas in Nürnberg.

After wandering in this area, take Kaiserstraße to the Fleischbrücke and cross the Pegnitz river, stopping to admire the view from the bridge. Just across the bridge, at Haupmarkt 2, is one of our favorite stores in Nürnberg, **Mobilia**. Mobilia is the best store we've found for modern furniture and "design" items. The store has recently expanded into the basement and top floor.

Leaving Mobilia, turn right and walk into the Hauptmarkt which on many days will be teeming with merchants selling fruits, vegetables, flowers, meats, sauerkraut, etc. Depending upon the time, you may want to move on to lunch — just a block away at the **Bratwursthäusle** — and then return to this square to shop or admire its two major attractions, the **Schöner Brunnen** and **Liebfraukirche**. (We suggest delaying lunch at the often crowded B'Häusle until after the midday rush.)

The Schöner Brunnen, located in the northwest corner of the square, was built in the fourteenth century. Legend has it that if you make a wish while turning the "journeyman's ring" at the base of the fountain, your wish will come true. Like nearly everything else you've seen, the fountain was rebuilt following the war and the 60 figures that make up the tiers are reproductions. The figures represent famous religious and civic figures, including Moses and the prophets at the top and the seven Electors around the bottom.

The Liebfraukirche has only recently come out from behind scaffolding while its clock was restored. At noon the clock puts on a little show.

The **Bratwursthäusle**, at Rathausplatz 1, is usually mobbed with tourists and locals alike. Nonetheless, you should brave the crowds in order to sample the spicy little bratwurst and tender *eisbein*. (Both come with sauerkraut, but if you prefer, you can substitute a very tasty potato salad.) There are no reservations and no waiting list. Circle the room, watching for people about to pay their bill. When you find a table about to be vacated, stay there until they leave and sit down immediately. Tables are shared here, so don't worry about sitting down at a table that is partially occupied.

After lunch, step next door into **St. Sebald's**. Pay special attention to the photos documenting the church's reconstruction — which was also a reconstruction of the city's pride and a testament to the resiliency of its residents.

From St. Sebald's walk up the hill on Bergstraße to the Beim Tiergärtner Tor, a pedestrian plaza at the top of the hill. If you have time, the **Kaiserburg**, Nürnberg's fifteenth century castle is to your right and affords some wonderful views of town. If not, travel left through this plaza to the **Albrecht Dürer House** on the corner.

The Dürer House is interesting, more because of its architecture and the glimpse it gives into how the artist lived and worked, than for its collection of the master's works. Far better collections of Dürer's works are on display at the Alte Pinakothek in Munich and the Albertina in Vienna.

Descend Albrecht Dürer Straße to the bottom, where a stairway will take you into Weinmarkt. Cross Weinmarkt and continue down the hill on Karlstraße. On your right, at Number 13, is the **Spielzugmuseum** (Toy Museum). Unfortunately, its fascinating displays have been moved out of town while the museum is remodeled. The temporary location is at 220 Sigmundstraße in the town of Weddis; take Furtherstrasse north to Sigmundstraße and turn left.

To return to the hotel, continue down Karlstraße, across the Karlsbrücke, turn right on Kaiserstraße, cross Josephsplatz and through the Ludwigplatz. Continue past the Hans-Sachs Brunnen, go left on Dr. Kurt Schumacher Straße, right on Jakobsplatz, then left on Knorrstraße. Enjoy a well-deserved cool beer in the Weinhaus Steichele's bar.

Wald und Schloßhotel Friedrichsruhe

#39

D-7111 Friedrichsruhe
West Germany
Telephone: 07941/7078
Singles 165DM to 175DM
Doubles 238DM to 278DM
Suites 388DM to 450DM
Major cards.

Few European country hotels can match the service found at the **Wald und Schloßhotel Friedrichsruhe**. Comfort and attention to detail are the watchwords of this beautiful castle hotel north of Stuttgart, near the town of Öhringen.

There are two main buildings at the hotel: the castle itself, built in 1712 as a hunting lodge for Johann Friedrich; and a newer building which houses the restaurant, lobby, a dozen or so guest rooms, suites and indoor swimming pool. The castle is an example of the early Baroque period that began in the late 17th century. The large entry hall is probably one of the few rooms still intact from when the building was used by royalty; both wings have since been divided into guest rooms which occupy most of three floors.

You will probably be most comfortable in the castle. It is separated from the newer structure and its activity — though you will have to walk through the weather on your way to dinner. (Management considered building a tunnel between the two buildings, but settled on leaving a supply of umbrellas near the doors of each.)

Guest rooms are beautiful. Our top recommendation is Number 66, a second floor corner room with a huge mahogany bed covered by the fluffiest eiderdown comforters we've had the pleasure of sleeping under, a beautiful dressing table with a tall mirror topped with a Greek pediment, high ceilings with ornate plaster detailing, a large bath and much more. Number 55 is also lovely, with two high mahogany beds and a large, comfortable sofa. Of the rooms in the main building, our favorite is Number 35.

Two other buildings on the grounds also have guest rooms: the *Jagdhaus*, which is also used for employee quarters; and the recently renovated *Torhaus*.

True to its heritage as a hunting lodge, activities at the Friedrichsruhe focus on the outdoors: there is a nine-hole golf course, tennis court, swimming pool (both indoor and outdoor) and walking trails nearby.

But it is service that sets this hotel apart. When we arrived, we found fresh-squeezed juice, mineral water and a bowl of fresh fruit waiting for us. The bath had extra towels plus large terry robes. When we returned to the room from dinner we found it had been cleaned, clothes folded and put away, the towels and robes replaced, the mineral water supply replenished and a plate of chocolates had been left. Our shoes were shined while we slept.

The Friedrichsruhe is somewhat isolated, so dining options are limited; but no matter, the hotel's restaurant is outstanding. As with the hotel, its strongest point is service. For example, we were handed the daily menu translated into English. Not unusual, we are English speakers and made our reservations in English. However, we were the only non-German diners and the menu contained about 40 items. We have concluded the entire daily menu was translated into English especially for us.

Another nice touch was the small folding card, illustrated with a watercolor by Johann Friedrich II, which listed what we had chosen for dinner that evening. This thoughtful token was sent to our table by head chef Lothar Eiermann along with his greetings and thanks.

Visit the Wald und Schloßhotel Friedrichsruhe in any season and enjoy a luxury retreat.

Hotel Bavaria

#40

Kienbergstraße 62
D-8962 Pfronten-Dorf
West Germany
Telephone: 08363/5004
Singles 98DM to 142DM
Doubles 180DM to 240DM
Apartments from 133DM per person
Major cards.

Summer and winter haven for a loyal cadre of upscale German holiday travelers, the **Bavaria** is one of those soothing, *gemütlich* hideaways that makes us want to extend our visit.

The chalet style building sits at the head of the valley floor at the base of a hill commanding a sweeping easterly view. On clear days there are even glimpses of the Zugspitze, towering over Garmisch-Partenkirchen, some 30 air miles away. Entire afternoons and evenings can be idled away on the hotel's wide terrace looking over the valley, reading a book or sunbathing. There are umbrella tables and efficient white-coated waiters to fetch whatever is needed.

The Bavaria has it all: a swimming pool that is part indoor, part outdoor (kept above 80 degrees in winter), Jacuzzi, sauna and massage. At its doorstep are hiking trails and cross-country and downhill skiing. The restaurant's food gets a toque from *Gault Millau*. Public rooms, full of fine furniture, rugs and heavy wood, are luxurious in the Bavarian style. Guest rooms are large, with plenty of extras, and most have balconies with views of the valley. What's more, the welcome is especially warm and visitors are close to Germany's best-known tourist attraction, the royal castles of Neuschwanstein and Hohenschwangau.

This would be a perfect spot to end a few days sightseeing on the Romantic Road, from Würzburg to Füssen. Whatever your travel itinerary, the Bavaria is just the sort of hotel to have waiting at the close of any day.

An Inexpensive Dining Alternative

If you don't wish to eat all your meals at the Bavaria, we recommend the down-to-earth **Hotel Post** in nearby Pfronten-Weißbach. What comes from the kitchen of its restaurant are major league portions of meat, potatoes, spätzle, dairy products and giant desserts.

If the American Heart Association published this book you no doubt would find something else to read in this space. But, since the AMA has other arteries to widen, we're going to tell you about the pan-fried calves liver heaped with bacon, and the venison ragout with spätzle and wild mushrooms. Liver in these parts is invariably better than what we find at home and at the Post it is extraordinary. Venison was also delicious, hearty and rich. The *gemischt salat* was just the way we like it, thinly-sliced vegetables and butter lettuce with a light dressing.

The restaurant is one huge barn-like room with great beams across the white plaster ceiling. There are white linen tablecloths and napkins. This is a place where the locals eat, where the waitresses are sturdy, friendly and competent.

Two beers, two mineral waters, salad and the liver and venison came to 48DM.

Schloß Hotel Spangenberg

#41

D-3509 Spangenberg
West Germany
Telephone: 05663/866
Singles 65DM to 150DM
Doubles 130DM to 230DM
Major cards except American Express.

Certain European hotels — like the Sacher in Vienna and the Vier Jahreszeiten in Hamburg — are approached with a sense of awe. Others are considered with a "we won't spend much time in the room anyway" sort of pragmatism. Then there are those few which generate that special feeling of excitement and anticipation that keeps us all traveling. Place the **Schloß Hotel Spangenberg** squarely in that category.

The hotel can be seen for several kilometers along the road to the small town of Spangenberg, some 20 miles southeast of Kassel. The Schloß sits at the pinnacle of the highest hill overlooking town. As you near this 13th century medieval fortress, follow the signs up the winding road to *Jagdschloß Spangenberg*. At the top, cross the drawbridge over the moat, pass under the clock tower keep and park in the stone courtyard.

The castle withstood a three-year siege during the 30-Years War, thanks in part to its supply of water from a well nearly 400 feet deep. It later served as the Spangenberg town prison, housed a school for foresters in the late 30s, and, during World War II, was used as an officer's prison camp. The fortress was damaged by Allied bombers in 1945, but has been painstakingly restored as a most appealing 26-room hotel.

Accomodations are large and comfortable. Our room had windows cut through the thick wall which overlooked the grassy moat — some 30 feet straight down the castle's facade — and the roofs of Spangenberg. Common areas feature polished hardwood floors, dark Oriental rugs and antique furnishings.

The restaurant, specializing in game dishes, is an inviting place with wood beamed ceiling, white walls and Gothic arches. You might also wish to consider making the 25 kilometer drive to Witzenhausen to dine at the excellent **Sommersberg Hotel**. This small, country inn serves high quality regional dishes at reasonable prices.

Switzerland

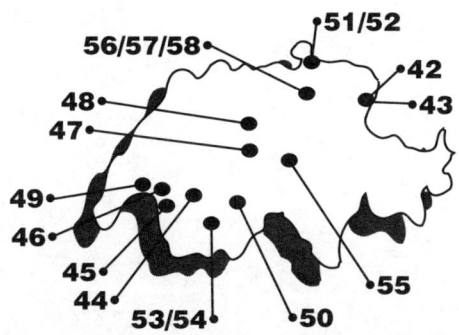

SWITZERLAND

42 Hotel Hecht
43 Romantik Hotel Säntis
44 Hostellerie Bon Accueil
45 Hotel Victoria
46 L'Auberge De Chernex
47 Chalet Du Lac
48 Landgasthof Hirschen
49 Hotel La Residence

50 Les Sources des Alpes
51 Hotel Chlosterhof
52 Hotel Rheinfels
53 Hotel de la Poste
54 Rosalp
55 Hotel Bären
56 Hotel Florhof
57 Hotel Tiefenau
58 Hotel zum Storchen

APPENZELL

The small Swiss canton of Appenzell combines all the elements we think make for a relaxing country holiday: fine, quiet hotels at good prices, excellent cuisine, beautiful scenery and friendly people. It is a land of green, rolling hills, intricately painted houses, and store signs of gilded wrought iron. Add to this the region's adherence to traditional customs and dress and you have the prototype for a *gemütlich* country vacation.

A fascinating side trip is to the nearby hamlet of Stein to the **Appenzeller Volksunde Museum**, where most mornings you can watch a farmer make Appenzell cheese the old way, by hand, over a wood fire. Then, walk next door to the **Schaukäserei** (showcase cheese dairy) and see the same process done by modern methods in gleaming stainless steel tanks, vats, centrifuges and presses — all computer-controlled.

Appenzell has a number of excellent small hotels, and we had trouble narrowing the list to two.

Hotel Hecht

#42

CH-9050 Appenzell
Switzerland
Telephone: 071/871025
Telex: 719267
Singles 70SF to 85SF
Doubles 110SF to 140SF
Major cards.

Compared with the other buildings on Appenzell's Hauptstraße, the facade of the **Hotel Hecht** is plain vanilla. Inside, too, it is simpler than the **Säntis**. But the Hecht is a hotel we would like to fold up, put in our suitcase and take with us from town to town.

There are few hotels where one is made to feel the way we do when at the Hecht: relaxed, comfortable and in the hands of professionals who know exactly what they are doing and are completely dedicated to caring for their guests.

Number 52, a delightful double room, is small but cozy, tucked up under the eaves with a view of the Alpsteins through a row of dormer windows. In the bathroom, we found plenty of storage space, a shower with seat, and extra towels.

Meals in the small, paneled dining room are excellent, with attentive friendly service and first-rate Swiss country cooking. Most entrees come with *rösti*, the tasty Swiss cottage-fried potatoes, and you can expect to receive second helpings of everything.

This 70-bed hotel has been in the Knechtle family for 50 years and since 1979 has been run by Maria and Regula Knechtle. At least one of these two will likely be present upon your arrival, at every meal, at check-out time and seemingly whenever needed for any reason.

Romantik Hotel Säntis

#43

CH-9050 Appenzell
Switzerland
Telephone: 030/883091
Telex: 71826
Singles 75SF to 90SF
Doubles 120SF to 160SF
Major cards.

The **Romantik Hotel Säntis** is the town's leading hotel and ideally situated on the historical *Landsgemeindeplatz* where the people of Appenzell gather each spring for public balloting. The front of the hotel, with its steep, gabled roof, rows of lace-curtained windows and intricately-painted facade overlooking the terrace, is an inviting scene.

Inside, heavy, dark beams, comfortable leather-upholstered furniture and marble floors reflect the affluence of the region. On one wall of the dining room is an impressive carved wood mural of life in Appenzell created in 1956 by local artist Hans Neff. Parts of the hotel, owned and run by generations of the Heeb family, have been recently renovated and it appears no expense was spared in obtaining the finest materials and fixtures.

Each of the three floors has its own color and design scheme, ranging from traditional to modern. The higher-priced doubles have small sitting rooms, and all rooms in the refurbished sections of the house have opulent glassed-in bathrooms. Doors and walls between the sleeping room and bathroom are floor-to-ceiling glass. A shade can be drawn for privacy. Bathroom interiors are white marble.

This is a luxurious, small (33 rooms) hotel, the "flagship" of the village of Appenzell.

CHÂTEAU-D' OEX

Château-d' Oex , part of the Swiss canton of Vaud, is an unpretentious village in the "pre-Alps" only a short drive or train ride from Montreux on Lac Léman (Lake Geneva). Actor David Niven was so captivated by the region he chose to live much of his life here and is buried in the town cemetery.

A tram journey to nearby Les Diableret Glacier is one of Europe's most spectacular ride-to-the-top-of-the-mountain-and-have-a-look-around spots. On a clear day one sees many of Europe's great peaks including the Matterhorn, the Jungfrau and Mont Blanc in France and, from the rickety deck of the Yeti Palace, some scary views straight down to the valley.

The restaurant at the summit serves a marvelous snack of *rebibes* , a style of *gruyere* unique to the Vaud. It is aged three years beyond the normal time and served dry and thinly sliced, with paper thin dried beef from Grisons. The meat and cheese is eaten with gherkins, tiny white onions and peppers. With the meal try a bottle of Yvorne, a white wine from Chasslais grapes. Be warned, though, this light wine of the Vaud slides down all too easily and at this altitude can be rather deadly.

The round trip to the glacier via three-stage cable car from Col du Pillon is about 35SF. The cable car from Reusch is the same price but you miss the steep leg of the journey.

Château-d' Oex is also the site each January of an important international ballooning competition. At any time of the year, however, you can hire — about $125 per person through the tourist office — a balloon to take you on a peaceful trip above the valley.

Also recommended is the **Musée du Vieux Pays d' Enhaut** in Château-d' Oex and its collection of intricate paper cuttings. This obscure craft is still alive and you will see these clever little *objets d' art* all over town.

Hostellerie Bon Accueil

MONTREUX

A recurring dream for many is some day living — at least part of the year — in Europe. In a what-would-you-do-if-you-won-$40-million-in-the-lottery sort of exercise, one can argue far into the night about where. Munich, Vienna or Berlin? Village or city? Town or country? Germany, Austria or Switzerland? How about France? It goes on and on. No conclusions have been reached but we recommend you put Montreux on your short list.

This city on lovely Lac Léman (don't say Lake Geneva) has many desirable qualities. It is an area of great physical beauty with a magnificent lake, mountains and an ever-changing sky; compelling scenery one never tires seeing.

We are not the first to recognize the attractions of this part of the world. Noel Coward had a house in the hills above Montreux and Charlie Chaplin lived out his years in nearby Vevey. Members of the Chaplin family are still there.

Even if you haven't won the lottery, at least devote a few days during your next European trip to Montreux.

Hotel Victoria

#45

CH-1823 Glion-sur-Montreux
Switzerland
Telephone: 021/9633131
Telex: 453102
Singles 60SF to 170SF
Doubles 150SF to 250SF
Major cards.

Our personal favorite among Montreux's hotels is the secluded **Hotel Victoria** in an extraordinary, wooded setting near the village of Glion in the hills about 1,000 feet above Montreux.

Its public rooms are a wonderful collection of Victorian era furniture, art objects, *bric a brac* and fine paintings. Don't miss the ancient barometer with its inked needle which traces a line on a drum to track the barometric pressure. In the hotel's bar are several museum quality paintings.

Off the lobby is the "winter garden" room with tiled floor, oriental rugs, wicker furniture and lots of indoor plants. In this sun room is an interesting scene of a village wine tasting painted by Eduard Ravel. The "blue" dining room's best feature is the excellent view across the lake to the Savoy Alps in France.

The Victoria's beautiful grounds contribute tremendously to the hotel's special atmosphere, that of a lovely private estate. Tables of the outdoor restaurant and terrace are scattered the length of the hotel — perhaps 50 yards — and have splendid views of the lake from beneath stately old trees and huge awnings that roll down from the side of the hotel. Just below the terrace is an outdoor heated pool which also has a lake view. Further beyond, in the trees, is the hotel tennis court.

No two of the 50 guest rooms are decorated alike. Antique pieces and original oil paintings abound. Materials such as wallpaper and carpeting are top quality. Daily, each room gets a supply of fresh flowers from the hotel's garden, plus mineral water and fresh fruit. Most rooms have excellent views.

Number 18 is a corner room with a door which opens to a terrace with lake and mountain views. Number 49 is large, almost two rooms, with an archway dividing the sitting and sleeping areas. There are two windows and a door to the terrace with a view across the vineyards toward Lausanne. There is a handsome game table in the center of the sitting area with inlaid chessboard, small couch, two overstuffed chairs around the game table, another comfortable chair and a writing desk with chair. The bathroom is nicely finished in burgundy tile and has tub, stall shower and double sink. Number 56 has lustrous mahogany furniture and a view of Chillon Castle and the mountains south of the lake.

The hideaway comfort of the Victoria makes it a good choice for longer stays. The hotel is a five-minute walk from the funicular to the lakeside and from there one can catch a bus for the five minute ride into the center of Montreux. The funicular runs at 15 minute intervals, the bus every 10 minutes. However, once settled in at the Victoria you just might not want to go anywhere for a few days.

L'Auberge De Chernex

#46

CH-1822 Chernex
Switzerland
Telephone: 021/9644191
Rooms 50SF per person
Major cards.

It has become increasingly difficult to find the kind of moderately-priced, charming little hotels run by caring, friendly folk that first drew many of us to Germany, Austria and Switzerland.

We are pleased to tell you of just such a place in the village of Chernex in the hills above Montreux. Robert Meier and Christine Demen opened **L'Auberge De Chernex** in July of 1988. It has a promising restaurant and seven cozy, spotless guest rooms. The place is almost a throwback, the kind one imagines expatriate writers and artists found in Europe during the '20s, with a street café where locals sit for hours over coffee or a glass of wine, a good restaurant, a few rooms upstairs and owners who know every customer.

A delightful decorating touch at L'Auberge De Chernex is a series of pretty little watercolors which hang on every wall and are the work of Robert Meier's mother. She began painting only a few years ago and does not normally sell her work, but if you like them you might inquire.

The seven guest rooms are small and simply decorated, only the four on the first floor (our second) have toilet and shower. All have twin beds except Number 1, which has a double bed ("*pour les amours*" is the way M. Meier delicately put it). The bathrooms are beautifully tiled floor-to-ceiling. Number 2 has a view across the street to a pretty little fountain, a garden and an old bakery. Number 3 is the largest room and has two windows with views of Montreux and the lake. Number 4 has just one window, is slightly smaller than Number 3, but with the same lake view. No two rooms are decorated or furnished alike.

The little dining room, comprising six to eight tables, has a clean look with white walls, light wood wainscoting, brass track-lighting, fresh flowers and more of Mme. Meier's watercolors. While the hotel seeks to be no more than a small, comfortable inn, its restaurant has its sights — and prices — set higher. Dinner for two with drinks and dessert will be in the 125SF to 175SF range.

We came away from L'Auberge De Chernex with the feeling its owners are people who not only want, but *know* how to do things right. Our guess is this place will soon be popping up in other guidebooks and travel magazines. There is much to recommend L'Auberge De Chernex: its location above the town, the inviting outdoor terrace with a view of Montreux and the lake, an already good restaurant that will get better, and comfortable guest rooms.

ISELTWALD

The best way to enjoy the spectacular show nature puts on around Interlaken is to avoid the crowded, touristy town between the lakes by staying in one of the region's small villages. One we like is a quiet, lakeside town which is secluded, yet close to Interlaken. More important, it has a small, immaculate hotel which would make a perfect base for excursions to the Kleine Scheidegg, the Schilthorn and the Jungfrau, and for exploring the many walking paths of the Bernese Oberland.

Chalet du Lac

#47

CH-3807 Iseltwald
Switzerland
Telephone: 036/451112
Singles 60SF to 75SF
Doubles 80SF to 134SF
Major cards.

On the south shore of the Brienzersee a narrow peninsula curves out from the lake shore, forming a protected bay some 200-300 meters across. The village of Iseltwald sits on this spit of land and the shore line across from it, making the shape of a "C." At the lower tip of this "C" is the **Chalet du Lac**, a quiet, 12-room gem of an inn directly on the lake, perhaps 10 meters from the shore, with its own small boat dock.

The Chalet du Lac has been a hotel for over 200 years. There once was a much larger building on the same site which served as the original hotel. Unfortunately, economic difficulties during two world wars led to its being disassembled in 1943, leaving only a restaurant and three rooms above it to be let to travelers.

But in 1985 the hotel was completely remodeled. The restaurant was turned into a *gäststube* and 12 rooms — including a family suite with loft — were built above it. A small structure connects this building with a cottage next door which formerly housed a group of woodcarvers.

Here a new restaurant and home for the proprietors, the Abegglen-Hohler family (whose son is the latest in a long line of hoteliers), was built.

The exterior of the hotel is standard Swiss chalet style: natural wood, peaked roofs, balconies with carved railings and flower boxes. In summer, the area in front of the house becomes a dining terrace with several umbrella-protected tables.

Though it has been four years since the hotel's renovation, you wouldn't know it to look at the rooms. They are so perfectly maintained they appear as new. Ten have lake views, nearly all have balconies large enough for a small table and chairs. All but two are different in size and layout, though each follows the same decorative scheme: light-colored knotty pine walls, white plaster ceilings and neutral beige carpets. Furnishings are constructed of a darker wood. Unlike many family-run hotels, where one often finds a mélange of chairs, desks and lamps, and towels and bedding in various colors, everything at Chalet du Lac matches; indicative, we think, of the precision and care with which Frau and Herr Abegglen-Hohler run their inn.

Do not expect a hearty, sit-a-spell-take-your-shoes-off-be-a-part-of-the-family welcome here, even though that's what one often finds at small country establishments like this. The Abegglen-Hohlers are polite and friendly, but more in the manner of a larger city hotel which provides efficient, but more reserved, service. Both speak fluent English.

What surprised us most about the Chalet du Lac was the quality of its restaurant. The specialty — not surprisingly — is fish; specifically *felchen*, a fresh water white fish. Iseltwald is one of the main fishing villages for the Interlaken area. Each morning, the five professional fishermen who live in Iseltwald head out with their nets and return with enough *felchen* to supply many of the area's restaurants. Based on our experience, they make sure the Chalet du Lac gets the best.

The one side dish not to be missed is Herr Hohler's version of *rösti*. Ordering this traditional Swiss dish brings a plate full of crispy potatoes with onions and bacon, topped with melted Emmenthal cheese. True "comfort" food.

The Chalet du Lac is better suited for those who enjoy directing their own activities or who prefer simply to sit on the terrace, reading a good book. For those seeking active but non-strenuous activities, the hotel offers a boat for rowing along the shore or perhaps out to the chapel on the small island near Iseltwald. Another favorite activity of guests here is the 2.5 kilometer (1.5 mile) walk along the shore to Giessbach and the Giessbach falls.

Iseltwald has little to offer in terms of night life. Walk through the town for half an hour and you've seen it all. The only building of architectural significance is the chateau at the tip of the peninsula which has been converted into an evangelical seminary and is in the process of being renovated. Yet, its central location in the Bernese Oberland and its quiet charm combine to make Iseltwald — and its top hotel, the Chalet du Lac — a highly recommended stop.

Recently the town was the backdrop for a Pan Am commercial. The Chalet du Lac's attractive terrace, with its view of the lake and the chateau, were used to sell the joys of European travel. It certainly made *us* want to go back.

Landgasthof Hirschen

Landgasthof Hirschen #48

CH-3350 Langnau im Emmental
Switzerland
Telephone: 035/21517
Singles 55SF to 75SF
Doubles 90SF to 130SF
Major cards.

In the prosperous little town of Langnau im Emmental is a tiny Swiss inn worth a detour from just about anywhere, especially if you are an American who loves wine. At the **Landgasthof Hirschen** you will find fine accommodations, excellent cuisine, a splendid wine cellar and an owner-chef-oenophile-raconteur in love with America and Americans.

The first license for serving wine at the Hirschen was granted to a Samuel Frisching in 1649. Since the late 1950s, the hotel has been owned and operated by Walter and Marla Birkhäuser. Frau Birkhäuser provides the warm welcome and sees that her 15-room hotel ticks with Swiss precision. Herr Birkhäuser is responsible for the cuisine and the late-night stories, shared with a bottle of wine around a table which holds the remains of wonderful meal.

Guest rooms at the Hirschen are well above the level of the average Swiss country inn. They are large and rustically decorated in light wood. The "bridal suite" is especially recommended for its beamed ceiling, canopy bed and split bath.

Walter Birkhäuser *looks* like a chef; bearded and burly with big mobile hands and the capable, energetic, but somewhat disheveled air of a male Julia Child. One gets the impression he does nothing by halves. As an example, his wine cellar contains some 15,000 bottles. One of his favorite stories involves the rescue of this cache when the hotel caught fire in 1983. Concerned his cellar would fill with the water used to fight the fire, Herr Birkhäuser — once assured his hotel guests were safe — disregarded all else in rescuing the wine. He quickly had two big water pumps going and was able to save nearly every bottle.

His food is traditional french, but not *nouvelle*, as Frau Birkhäuser is quick to say. His *rösti* is among the best we've ever had. (The secret, he says, is to let the potatoes sit for a few days after boiling and to fry them in lard.)

The Emmental is one of Switzerland's loveliest regions, and the Landgasthof Hirschen is one of its best country inns.

LAUSANNE

Lausanne, the capital of the French-speaking canton of Vaud, is built on a series of hills overlooking lovely Lac Léman (natives are said to be offended when it is referred to as Lake Geneva). Levels of the city are connected by a funicular. In the old part of the city, high above the lake, a town crier still calls the night hours. It is a cosmopolitan city, with many fine hotels, shops and restaurants.

Hotel La Residence #49

Place du Port 15
CH-1000 Lausanne 6
Switzerland
Telephone: 021/277711
Telex: 24605
Singles 130SF to 170SF
Doubles 190SF to 250SF
Major cards.

Adjoining Le Beau Rivage Palace, one of the world's great hotels, and sharing its nice proximity to the lake, is **La Residence**, a hotel of three buildings in French Regency style named Lutetia, Florissant and Platane. The grounds are most attractive and there is an outdoor pool. The separate buildings and the pleasant grounds give La Residence a country inn feel.

Of the 48 guest rooms we particularly like Number 2, a large corner room with three windows, two of which look out at the lake. There are two soft chairs, a sofa, coffee table and an oversize television. Another double, Number 207, was too small for our taste and had no view, but Number 209 was a comfortable single. Bathrooms have floor-to-ceiling tile, hair dryers, a few come with double sinks and all are spotlessly clean.

The hotel makes a good first impression with a light and airy reception area tiled in black and white marble, handsome fireplace and armloads of fresh flowers.

Though the guest rooms don't quite match the hotel's location, the charming buildings and grounds, we recommend it above any other four-star in Lausanne.

GREAT DINING IN LAUSANNE'S *ALTSTADT*

The best restaurant in Lausanne is Angélika and Peter Baermann's **La Grappe d' Or** in the old town. A meal there is a revelation of the region's fine cooking and a demonstration of the difference in food when one ventures south of Switzerland's *Rösti* border, that imaginary Swiss version of the Mason-Dixon line which marks German-speaking from French-speaking Switzerland.

One difference became clear to us near the end of the meal. The Germans, Austrians and Swiss are first-rate cheese makers and cheese eaters. But in most of their restaurants one does not encounter that most civilized of gustatory customs — the cheese cart. We think we get good cheese in the San Francisco Bay Area and take pride in our numerous fine stores and restaurants. But the La Grappe d' Or let us know again how really good cheese — made within a few kilometers of the restaurant — can be. *Brie* in California has become a cliche, too often an ammoniated, gooey triangle found at every cocktail party. But an ounce of *brie* off the cart at La Grappe d' Or will make you question whether you have ever eaten a food by that name. All the other cheeses we selected were equally good.

Two fish courses – turbot and salmon – on the shorter fixed-price menu (87SF) were exquisite. Both were perfectly cooked, just underdone, and the salmon came with a sauce made from fresh grapefruit and butter reduced with the scrapings from the pan. After devouring the fish course, we thought we had scaled the heights to which La Grappe d'Or can climb. We were wrong. Medallions of lamb with five spices in a light curry sauce took us to a new level.

After the meal, try a speciality of the house, *Resinet*, an indescribable creamy, wine tart in flaky pastry. Combine that with the cheese and fresh raspberries topped with thick cream and shaved white chocolate in pastry and all the rest, you have the ingredients for a memorable meal.

We drank wines from the Vaud and found them a delight. At this and other restaurants in the region we drank white wine made from the Chasselais grape. One, Dezaley, is said to be the best wine of the Lavaux wine region. These white wines are always fresh and never seem to tire the palate as the inexpensive wines of California sometimes do. The red wine drunk with the lamb was a 1985 Pinot Noir by La Maison Carreé Auvernier, a light wine in the Beaujolais style.

La Grappe d' Or, 3 Cheneau-de-Bourg, 1003 Lausanne, telephone (021) 23 07 60. Dinner for two with wine will start at about 175SF.

Les Sources des Alpes

#50

CH-3954 Leukerbad
Switzerland
Telephone: 027/621151
Telex: 472009
Fax: 027 61 35 33
Singles 215 SF to 470 SF
Doubles 300 SF to 520 SF
Half board is 76 SF
Major cards.

In 1985, at the tender age of 29, Rene Isler, an engineer-turned-innkeeper, and his wife, Francoise, sold their small hotel in the Grisons and headed for Leukerbad, a small, spa town above the Rhone valley on the southern slopes of the Swiss Alps. There they convinced the town fathers to invest $10 million in a scheme to turn a nicely located but rather venerable, nondescript hotel into one of Europe's premier hide-aways.

With an attention to detail intense even by Swiss standards, the Islers appear to have pulled it off. **Les Sources des Alpes** makes it big in virtually every category: quiet, beautiful setting; exquisite guest and public rooms; a friendly staff who quickly and cheerfully provides a vast range of services, and a restaurant that delivers delicious, creative meals.

The outdoor pool, tucked into a hill next to a little grove of trees and heated to 90 degrees with a frothy spa in one corner, is restful and inviting. A rock wall and clear plastic canopy protect the 15 or so comfortable chaises gathered round it. While paddling in the warm water and gratefully contemplating the twists and turns of life that delivered you to this spot at this time, lift your eyes to the sheer rock faces that cut the sky 3,000 feet straight above. They enclose the town on three sides and provide its spectacular setting. On late summer afternoons you can watch a thunder storm gather behind the wall and begin to move over the town. There's plenty of time to escape to your room, however, for a pre-dinner nap while it blows over. Naturally, when you get out of the pool — *every time* you get out of the pool — someone is there to wrap a large heated towel around your shoulders. The nap and summer storm are just the ticket for ensuring an appetite.

Which brings us to the hotel's restaurant, **La Malvoisie**. Chef Patrick Burger was lured by Isler to preside over the hotel's gleaming, high-tech kitchen. The result is wonderful food, imaginatively prepared, course after course, meal after meal.

After one or two meals at La Malvoisie one begins to feel the excitement such cuisine can engender. We looked forward to each new course like an enthralled audience awaits the next baffling trick of a great magician. *Poularde en vessie demi-deuil* (for two persons) brought a large roasted Bresse chicken. First the breast was carved and served with a buttery truffle sauce we won't even attempt to describe. While we ate the white meat, the legs and wings were returned for additional cooking and a short time later constituted a second service. Served with the chicken were shiny little skillets of small wild mushrooms, lightly sauteed, and a small dish of perfectly steamed spinach. The latter, of course, was grown in the hotel's garden in nearby Sion. One dinner began with a dollop of avocado mousse in pastry followed immediately by a tiny sliver of fish in a sauce of spicily sauteed yellow, red, and green peppers. Another began with a refreshingly cool melon soup. Each day, superb rolls and breads are not only baked on the premises, the grain is ground there as well.

None of the dishes was heavy and even those with the richest ingredients maintained a lightness that avoided the kind of postprandial feelings so well-depicted in Alka-Seltzer commercials.

Desserts, too, were imaginative and delicious. A good example was a warm rhubarb tartlette with fresh cream and clear gelatin to counter the sourness of the rhubarb. Naturally, the restaurant makes its own ice creams and sorbets. A selection of the latter — the containers are brought to the table and you point as with the cheese cart — makes for a superb, low-calorie dessert. But even if you escape this course calorically unscathed there is still a plate of delectable little sweets to be negotiated.

M. Isler is an enthusiastic oenophile and the wine list shows it. The card goes far beyond the standard repertoire. But only a wine *aficianado* — and a well-heeled one at that — would even consider spending 3000 SF ($1800) for the '45 Château d'Yquem. The rest of us will be satisfied with the local wines of the Vaud and Valais, which are of high quality and far more affordable. There is a wide selection of both white and red in the 35 SF ($21) to 45 SF ($27) range. If you don't want an entire bottle there are good wines served by the glass.

After dinner it's time to toddle across the lobby to the wood paneled bar, sink into a comfortable couch or chair and enjoy the final beverage of the evening while listening to the gleaming grand piano.

Breakfast also demonstrates the hotel's commitment to excellence. Coffee is brewed to order in a Melior pot for each table; boiled eggs are served in a ceramic coddler so there are no shells to deal with; the orange juice is fresh-squeezed and the wonderful jams and jellies — you guessed it — are housemade.

Guest rooms are quiet, well equipped and beautifully decorated in a modern, clean style. The Islers say creating a good hotel is dealing with thousands of details. At Les Sources they appear to have seen to most of them. Furnishings, fabrics and fixtures were all specially made for the hotel. Colors have been chosen for their subtlety and relaxing qualities. Every bathroom has a window, a clear glass-enclosed shower, separate large tub and separate room for toilet and bidet. Naturally, there are terry robes and comfortable sandals for the spa and pools. The pipes for each bathroom's plumbing fixtures are independent of all other rooms. Thus you never awaken to the sound of rushing water when the guest above or next to you turns on the shower. We heard nothing but the wind in the trees at night.

Rooms and floors are named, not numbered. The house's best is the *Abricot* suite. Its' two rooms plus large bath are spread over 750 square feet. White ceilings are low. Heavy white drapes and white sheers hanging from brass rods, frame the three windows and two french doors, both of which lead to their own small balcony. Door and window frames are snowy white with brass fixtures. Other rooms are smaller but just as well appointed.

For most, this is a hotel for the special occasion. The *Abricot* suite is 520 SF with breakfast or 672 SF half-board. At the other end of the price spectrum are the smallest rooms — 360 square feet — for 215 SF single and 300 SF double, both with breakfast. If you stay 10 days or more, the price drops between 5% and 10%. Even at these prices Les Sources offers excellent value. The restaurant, while fairly priced when compared with others in its class, could not be said to be a bargain, however. Though you will pay less than at Aubergine in Munich or at Crissier, or the best restaurants in New York, and about the same as top restaurants in California, a trypical three course dinner for two without wine will cost nearly 200 SF.

Les Sources des Alpes offers a splendid combination of cuisine and accommodations and deserves a spot in the front rank of small European country hotels. It is a place to let calories and dollars be numbers accounted for at another time and another place. Whether you go for a month each year, a few days each trip or one day once in a lifetime, it will be a memorable experience.

STEIN AM RHEIN

Switzerland's most northerly canton, Schaffhausen, juts out from the rest of the country, an island in a sea of Germany. It is a wine making region which produces mostly Pinot Noir and Riesling. As with much of the Swiss countryside, its principal attractions are miles of walking paths, quiet villages and an abundance of natural beauty. In this instance, the quiet village is Stein am Rhein, population 2500.

Stein am Rhein is a medieval town, filled with old half-timbered houses, many intricately painted, some with oriel windows.

Two hotels in the village deserve to be included here.

Hotel Chlosterhof

#51

CH-8260 Stein am Rhein
Switzerland
Telephone: 054/424242
Fax: 054 41 13 37
Telex: 897058
Singles 120SF to 150SF
Doubles 160SF to 210SF
Major cards.

The **Chlosterhof**, which opened in 1986, is a good example of how a modern building can enhance a medieval town. Located just outside the gathering of ancient structures which comprise this river village's *altstadt*, the hotel keeps a profile as low as its neighbors, rising only four floors to a sawtooth roofline. The exterior is principally red brick with dark wood trim. Rather than trying to mimic the antiquity of its neighbors, the architects instead designed it to fit with the surroundings while maintaining its modern feel.

The entry and lobby are breathtaking. Vaulted white ceilings arch over floors of glistening red Italian marble. Here and there are massive pieces of richly-carved wood antiques, including a spectacular Baroque armoire whose value was described to us as approximating that of a Mercedes-Benz 500 SEC.

Ingeniously, all 68 rooms have views of the Rhine. Many have fireplaces and 10 have four-poster beds. All are spacious and luxuriously furnished. Some are townhouse style with a short stairway to a sleeping area above, a toilet on each level and 15-foot-plus floor-to-ceiling windows which overlook the river. Bathrooms have marble floors, tile walls and cabinets jammed with every conceivable complimentary cosmetic.

Number 308 is a corner suite which could accommodate two couples or a family of four or five. It has a fireplace, terrace over the river, numerous river-view windows and a small kitchen with dishwasher. Number 401 would also be an excellent choice.

The hotel's elegant **Le Bateau** restaurant rates a red *toque* from *Gault Millau* and offers main dishes in the 25-45SF range. Its wine list is extensive.

The Chlosterhof also has a sauna, solarium, well-equipped workout room and a beautiful, small, indoor swimming pool. Covered parking is provided at no charge to guests.

Hotel Rheinfels

#52

CH-8260 Stein am Rhein
Switzerland
Telephone: 054 41 21 44
Singles from 65SF to 100SF
Doubles from 120SF to 180SF
No cards.

What the Chlosterhof does in a shiny new way, the nearby **Rheinfels** does in a shiny old way.

Once a storage building for salt being transported on the river, the Rheinfels has recently been beautifully refurbished. Remaining are the venerable beams, the creaky but highly-polished 18-inch floor planks in some of the common areas, and thick walls which taper from seven meters thick at the foundation to a single meter at the roof line. A few of the giant beams, which date from 1400, now get extra support from steel girders.

In the refurbishment process, owner/chef Edi Schwegler has created an inn with tremendous appeal. A number of new guest rooms were added and what one guidebook described as "seven adequate rooms" is now 20 charmers, all on the river.

Number 32 is a lovely large double with low, beamed ceiling and windows opening onto the Rhine. Though second-floor rooms such as Number 24 don't have the ancient beams, the fact that they are a bit lower puts the river right outside your window. Most rooms are large enough for a sitting area and writing desk; walls are covered by attractive wallpaper in the Biedermeier style with an intricate flower pattern. The immaculate bathrooms have floor-to-ceiling tile. Guestroom furnishings are more traditional than at the Closterhof, with dark — but not heavy — wood predominating.

The Rheinfels is full of nice touches, such as antique furniture and Oriental rugs in the public rooms. A full suit of armor stands in one hall.

Herr Schwegler is as good a cook as he is *hotelier*. The French kitchen emphasizes fish from the Rhine and nearby Lake Constance

Hotel Rheinfels

(Bodensee). We tried *frito misto* and the grilled salmon, and can recommend both. A huge awning covers a large terrace on the river providing outdoor dining in all but the coldest weather.

Finally, the Rheinfels is a marvelous bargain.

THE RESTAURANT SCENE

While in the Schaffhausen/Stein am Rhein area, plan to eat at least one meal at the **Schloß Taverne Herblingen**. The restaurant is in the converted carriage house of an historic walled fortress. Peacocks roam the grounds. The interior decor, with its collection of doll houses and the massive stone fireplace, make the Herblingen worth a visit even if the kitchen served nothing but hot dogs. But, given that the kitchen produces good, traditional Swiss cuisine, with an emphasis on local fish and game, the Schloß Taverne Herblingen is a must stop. Expect to spend between 120 and 240 SF for two for dinner.

Also in the region are two restaurants included in most "Best of Switzerland" lists: the chic, pricey little **Fischerzunft** and the even tinier **Restaurant Sonne**. The Sonne is in Stein am Rhein, the Fischerzunft in Schaffhausen.

Finally, it is imperative that you make the short drive (39 kilometers - 24 miles) across the German border to Donaueschingen in order to sample what we believe is the best pastry known to man: **Original Hengstler Bienenstich**, available only at the **Café Hengstler** at Number 45 Karlstraße. Describing this delicious sweet is difficult, but we shall try. The base is a layer of flaky, buttery shortbread about half an inch thick. This is topped with approximately an inch of heavy cream, whipped to the point where it is almost as stiff as soft butter. Next comes another layer of shortbread crowned by a quarter-inch thick layer of carmelized sliced almonds. It sounds simple, but tastes sublime. And you can have it for 2.70DM. Who knew admission to heaven was such a bargain?

Switzerland

VERBIER

Not so many years ago Verbier was a sleepy Swiss village, sitting on a sunny plateau in the French-speaking canton of Valais. No one paid much attention to this little town where cows outnumbered people. But some of the farmers realized the mountains which rose above the town were good for something other than summer grazing grounds and formed a consortium to develop Verbier as a world-class Alpine resort. Verbier has become just that, though relatively few Americans have discovered it.

Skiing is fantastic, with plenty of terrain for every level of skier, from beginner to Olympian. More than 80 lifts are served by one lift ticket, but be careful: it's easy to get lost and find yourself quite a distance from home at the end of the day. Buses will take you back to Verbier, but you might be in for a long ride. For non-skiers, Verbier also offers hiking in summer, plus a modern sports center with ice rink, squash courts, Olympic-size indoor pool, etc.

Hotel de la Poste

#53

CH-1936 Verbier
Switzerland
Telephone: 026/75681
Telex: 473357
Singles 74SF to 126SF
Doubles 134SF to 228SF
Prices are half-board
Major cards.

Don't be alarmed if you think you see Walter Mondale greeting guests at the **Hotel de la Poste** — it's not really the former VP, just proprietor Serge Putallaz-Oreiller. Take a minute to introduce yourself when you arrive and he'll probably drop by your table each night at dinner to say hello. But don't praise the cooking too much or a second helping may appear in front of you and your waistline could suffer. On Monday or Tuesday night, Serge fires up the *raclette* grill and most of his guests gather at a long table to eat this Valaisian specialty of melted *Bagne* cheese with boiled potatoes and gherkins and drink copious amounts of *Fendant*, the light wine of the region.

The Poste is simply furnished, clean and amazingly quiet for being on the main street of Verbier (not a thouroughfare by any means, but still one of the most heavily traveled streets in town). Though comfortable enough, it is better suited for those who ski or hike or play tennis; those who want to relax and read in their rooms would be better off at the Rosalp.

Breakfast and dinner are included in your room rate, making the Poste a fine bargain. The kitchen turns out what one guest described as "home cooking — but the kind of home cooking that's reserved for special guests on Sunday evenings."

While you are in Verbier, you might want to have lunch one day at **Offshore**, on Rue de Médran, just steps from the Médran lift. Offshore is like a little bit of Malibu: a hot pink VW bug with a surfboard sticking out of its rear window dominates the restaurant and the surfing motif is used throughout. A loud, young crowd comes to Offshore for the excellent salad bar and perfect french fries.

Rosalp

#54

CH-1936 Verbier
Switzerland
Telephone: 026/76323
Telex: 473322
Singles 140SF to 240SF
Doubles 277SF to 420SF
Prices are half-board
Major cards.

The **Rosalp** is Verbier's finest hotel. With just 14 rooms and ten luxury apartments, but a staff numbering more than fifty, the Rosalp is prepared to meet your every need. Like many great country hotels, the Rosalp feels more like a comfortable home than a hotel: the sofa in your room was purchased because it fit perfectly under the alcove window, not because it could be ordered by the dozen. Although the rooms are small, they are quite comfortable and baths are large. Madame Pierroz runs her hotel with typical Swiss precision but still extends a warm welcome, especially to returning guests.

People come to Verbier for one of two reasons: either to ski or to eat at the Rosalp, which is one of the country's top restaurants. Chef Roland Pierroz's cuisine has been grouped with that of countryman Fredy Girardet and Frenchman Paul Bocuse. Heady company, but the comparisons are deserved, his cooking is superb. Though everything is wonderful, don't miss his fish dishes or desserts. Expect to spend from $50 to $100 per person, depending upon how much you indulge yourself. Of course, if you go on a shopping spree in the 40,000-bottle wine cellar, that total could go up rapidly.

Hotel Bären

CH-3812 Wilderswil
Switzerland
Telephone: 036/22521
Telex: 923137
Fax: 036/223544
Singles 54 SF to 77 SF
Doubles 92 SF to 132 SF
Major cards.

Not far from the touristy bustle of Interlaken, is the village of Wilderswil and many frequent travelers' Swiss home away from home, the unpretentious **Hotel Bären**. Year after year the Bären's clientele repeats, not only Britsh and Americans, of which there are many, but from all over the world, including Switzerland.

The reasons for such loyalty are obvious and begin with the Bären's management. Low-key, friendly, efficient and seemingly tireless, Fritz Zurschmiede is likely to grab new guests by the elbow and take them on a walking tour of the town where he and his family have lived and operated their hotel for generations. To spend a few minutes around Herr Zurschmiede watching the way he deals with his employees and his guests, is to understand one of the major reasons for the success of his hotel.

The four story Bären dominates one corner of Wilderswil's tiny town *platz*. It's a typical Swiss building, a hotel that looks like hundreds of others: peaked roof, green shutters, red geraniums boiling out of flowerboxes and a small terrace with brightly colored tables and umbrellas. Inside are most of the hotel's approximately 40 guest rooms (across the street in another building are a few interesting guest rooms furnished with antiques and decorated in the style of 100 years ago) and its three restaurants: a rustic pub which serves hearty Swiss fare, a pizza parlor and a more upscale room with linen napery and fine glassware. Each has a different following and each, in its way, is an important gathering spot for the residents of Wilderswil, which, of course, is the best possible recommendation.

Though the building is old (there has been a licensed hotel on these premises since 1706) its heart is a gleaming, stainless steel kitchen loaded with 1990s high tech gadgets. The food it produces is excellent.

Breakfast at the Bären, included in the room price, is as good as we have ever eaten at a hotel of this category. In addition to the huge selection of cheeses, meats, juices, pastries, breads, cereals, fresh fruit, jam and jellies, is a chef stationed at the buffet table who cooks eggs to order.

Bedrooms at the Bären are typical Swiss country; moderate in size, rough wood and plain furnishings. Most have TV, radio and mini-bar. Some on the south side have views of the the great mountains; the Eiger, Mönch and Jungfrau. In the hotel's newer section each room has a small balcony. Everything is spotless and well maintained.

This is a place you might walk into for the first time and ask yourself, "What's the big deal?" The big deal is the service, the genuine regard in which management seems to hold its guests, the small-town atmosphere and the way you will quickly begin to feel right at home.

ZÜRICH

Like Paris, Zürich is divided by a river whose left and right banks have distinctly different personalities. Here though, the positions are reversed. Paris' left bank is home to the University and the funky-chic neighborhoods, shops and restaurants; in Zürich, the University is on the right bank of the Limmat, financial institutions and more upscale shopping on the left. On the left you will find Yves Saint Laurent, Cartier, Bucherer, Armani, Versace and other high-end outlets. On the right, art galleries and antique shops.

The left is restaurants where standard traveler's wear (comfortable walking shoes, no ties or skirts, etc.) is only grudgingly accepted. The right is cafes where you feel the energy of youth. The left bank rolls up the sidewalks relatively early and there are few people on the streets; on the right you will find crowds strolling the narrow, hilly streets late into the evening.

In other words, decide what mood you are in and visit the side of the river where you feel most comfortable. Or change your outlook on life simply by walking across a bridge.

Zürich is a good walking city, the center is compact, many streets are pedestrian only and most major sights are within easy walking distance of the hotels reviewed here. Because it attracts so many business people on expense accounts, the city is not cheap, but it is no more expensive than other major European cities. As you might expect, the better values are on the right bank.

Hotel Florhof

#56

Florhofgasse 4
CH-8001 Zürich
Switzerland
Telephone: 01/474470
Telex: 817364
Singles 105SF to 145SF
Doubles 165SF to 210SF
Major cards.

The welcome at the **Hotel Florhof** is the warmest you will find in Zürich. Herr Schilter is a hotelier who truly loves his job. He trained at Swiss Hotel School and worked in larger establishments before a friend, who had purchased the hotel in 1925, asked him to run it. That was 30 years ago. Herr Schilter is still there.

The blue stuccoed five-story building with white shuttered windows first appeared on Zürich town plans in 1576. The first owner of record was Zürich politician Hans Heinrich Hofmann. In the early 1700s, Captain Jakob Oeri — who became one of the town's first millionaires — bought the house and it remained in his family until 1811. Some original pieces of furniture from this rich history remain and are displayed in the halls and common areas. Doorways to the rooms are dark, heavy wood set in wood archways — reproductions of doors that existed when the Florhof was built.

Rooms are good-sized, spotlessly clean and simply-decorated. Our favorite is Number 22, which is the only room which retains the plaster detailing on the ceiling. Some rooms have pleasant views of Zürich, and all are quiet, thanks to the hotel's location on a narrow street just off the Hirschengraben. Not all rooms have television, but if there is something you must see the staff will bring one to your room.

Parking is difficult in this neighborhood. Leave your keys with the front desk, though, and they will store your car in a nearby lot. The hotel has use of this lot only at night, but not to worry — come morning they'll move it to safe street parking for you.

Reserve well in advance, the Florhof has a large clientele of regulars who return year after year. The hotel's restaurant has a good reputation, and the dining room is small but comfortable. Note the parquet walls: they used to be the floors when the hotel was a private home.

Hotel Tiefenau

Steinwiesstraße 8-10
CH-8032 Zürich
Switzerland
Telephone: 01/2518246 (reservations only)
Fax: 01/2512476
Telex: 816395
Singles from 130SF to 190SF
Doubles from 190SF to 290SF
Major cards.

In a neighborhood of fine homes on the right bank, close enough to town to be convenient yet quiet enough to be a pleasant retreat, is the **Hotel Tiefenau**. Nestled among beautiful old birch trees and a lovely garden, the Tiefenau would make an excellent choice for an extended stay.

The house was built in 1835 and slowly converted to use as a hotel. No two rooms are the same size or shape, nor do they have the same furnishings. The exterior is a pale yellow stucco with grey shuttered windows. A yellow and white striped awning extends over the entry, which leads to a small lobby and hallway linking the two wings of the hotel.

The atmosphere at the Tiefenau is very much that of a home away from home. The staff goes out of its way to make guests feel at ease, and the house is set up for relaxed living: overstuffed chairs in the sitting areas, quiet nooks with books and magazines set out, etc.

You will be quite comfortable at the Tiefenau.

Hotel zum Storchen #58

Am Weinplatz 2
CH-8001 Zürich 22
Switzerland
Telephone: 01/2115510
Fax: 01/2116451
Telex: 813354
Singles 160SF to 240SF
Doubles 260SF to 360SF
Major cards.

The **Hotel zum Storchen** is directly on the Limmat, facing the Weinplatz. This location is the Storchen's most attractive feature. Though it is in the middle of all the action in Zürich, rooms are quiet. On one side of the Storchen is the river and on two other sides are pedestrian walkways. The fourth side is the Weinplatz, which carries little traffic.

Most of the rooms have been renovated recently. The restored rooms are modern but not austere and, overall, among the most attractive in town, though they lack the personality one might expect from an establishment with over 600 years of history. We recommend you ask for Number 524, a top floor corner room with a small balcony with views of the River, the Grossmünster church, the Zürichsee and, on a clear day, the Alps. Single rooms here are especially nice — not large, but well-appointed.

Service is about average for a big city hotel, quite attentive but slightly aloof. The Storchen is an excellent choice for those shopping in the myriad of stores in the neighborhood, or merely as a central base for sightseeing. However, one will pay for this location.

A ZÜRICH WALKING TOUR

Zürich, like many European cities, was settled long before the term "city planning" was invented. While this makes driving a little more difficult, it also gives the city that sense of romance, quaintness and accessibility so many travelers seek. (Don't let us deter you from entering the city by car: the Swiss are good drivers and the streets clearly marked. This is not Florence or Rome.)

This walk is meant to provide an overview of the major sights and attractions of Zürich. Depending upon how quickly you walk and how much time you choose to spend in the churches and museums along the way, this stroll could last anywhere from three hours to three days. If you take it at a relatively leisurely pace and leave the two museums for another day, you can complete the walk in a day and still enjoy a relaxed lunch. It's easy to get turned around in Zürich, so you'll find it helpful to purchase a detailed street map. When all else fails, orient yourself by the major churches; their steeples will guide you on your journey.

We begin at the door of our favorite hotel in Zürich, the **Florhof**. Walk down Florhofgasse to Hirschengraben and turn immediately left onto Heimstraße. You'll see the tram tracks and will follow the path taken by the number 31 train. In about two blocks you will be at Heimplatz and the **Kunsthaus**.

The Kunsthaus concentrates on work from the 19th and 20th centuries, though you will find earlier works here as well. Last winter the museum held a retrospective of the work of Edvard Munch, but even without a special showing there are more works here by Munch than in any museum outside the artist's native Scandinavia. You will also find more than a dozen works by Marc Chagall and an entire wing is devoted to the Swiss-born artist Giacometti.

When you have seen your fill in this very well-designed space for art, return the way you came, up Heimstraße to where it becomes Seilergraben. Turn immediately left into the Neumarkt, which quickly becomes a pedestrian-only street. As you stroll down Neumarkt (becomes Rindermarkt), you will be walking past some of Zürich's most interesting shops. At Neumarkt 2, you will find the **Restaurant zur Kantorei**, a wonderful little place for lunch which offers good food and excellent service. Ask for a table near the windows and you can watch the Zürich right-bank crowd go by.

You might find it enjoyable to explore this area on your own for a bit. When you are ready, walk towards the river until you reach Niederdorfstraße/Münstergasse. The **Restaurant Turm**, just off the Münstergasse at Obere Zäune 19 is also an excellent lunch stop.

Follow Münstergasse until you reach Zwingliplatz and the Grossmünster. The church was built sometime between the 11th and 13th centuries on the site of a church said to have been founded by Charlemagne. In the crypt you will find a huge statue of a seated Charlemagne, a sword across his knees. The Grossmünster also boasts a collection of lovely stained glass windows by Giacometti.

Walk down the stairs to the river and cross the **Münsterbrücke**. You are now outside the **Fraumünster**. The main attraction of this slightly smaller church is a collection of stained glass windows by Chagall. The best time to see these east-facing windows is before noon.

The plaza on the north side of the Fraumünster is the **Münsterhof**, formerly Zürich's pig market. At the northeast corner of the Münsterhof is where the Storchengasse, another pedestrian-only street, begins. There are several rather exclusive shops in this neighborhood. Incidentally, that huge clock face on the tower to your left is the largest clock face in Europe — no less than we'd expect from the Swiss. The church is **St. Peter's**.

The Storchengasse leads to Weinplatz. The narrow way leading out of this small square is Rennweg. Follow it a short distance (perhaps 200 meters) until you reach a set of stairs leading away to your right. At the top of these stairs is a tiny park called the **Lindenhof**. Because it affords such an excellent view of the river, it was the original site of the Celtic and Roman settlements that eventually became Zürich. Quite often you will find old men playing chess with two foot-high playing pieces.

Go down the stairs at the other side of the Lindenhof and walk down the narrow Lindenhofstraße. At Number 7 is the jewelry workshop of Robert Hegar and Rainer Berchtold. Their tiny shop produces some very lovely modern and classically-styled pieces. At Oetenbachgasse turn left until you reach the Bahnhofstraße.

Zürich's most famous street, the Bahnhofstraße is at its best here, in the last few blocks before it reaches the Hauptbahnhof. The street is lined with shops, a couple of delicatessens and, of course, banks.

Walk to the train station and around its east side, finally turning left onto Museumstraße. On your right will be the **Schweizerisches Landesmuseum** (Swiss National Museum) with its eight-story tower sporting a multi-colored tile roof. This collection of buildings is one of the most enjoyable museum visits a European traveler can make. The exhibits — which represent a cross-section of the art, culture and history of the country — are clearly and attractively presented. The staff couldn't be more friendly and, best of all, admission is free.

If you have any energy left, you might want to walk along the river to the Zürichsee. Stay on the left bank, the walk is much quieter. Or, if your feet can't handle another block, jump on a Number 4 tram, take it across the river and change at the "Central" stop to a Number 3 or Number 31. This will take you to the intersection of Seilergraben and Florhofgasse .